# Mad Cowboy

## Plain Truth from the Cattle Rancher Who Won't Eat Meat

## HOWARD F. LYMAN

*with*

## GLEN MERZER

*This book is the work of Howard Lyman and Glen Merzer.*
*The publication of this book is not affiliated with,*
*nor endorsed by, the Humane Society*
*of the United States.*

A TOUCHSTONE BOOK
PUBLISHED BY SIMON & SCHUSTER
NEW YORK   LONDON   TORONTO   SYDNEY   SINGAPORE

For Willow Jeane with love

TOUCHSTONE
Rockefeller Center
1230 Avenue of the Americas
New York, NY 10020

TOUCHSTONE and colophon are registered trademarks of
Simon & Schuster, Inc.

Designed by Colin Joh
Text set in Baskerville

Manufactured in the United States of America

5   7   9   10   8   6   4

The Library of Congress has cataloged the Scribner edition as follows:
Lyman, Howard F.
Mad cowboy: plain truth from the cattle rancher who won't eat
meat/Howard F. Lyman, with Glen Merzer.
p.   cm.
1. Vegetarianism. 2. Meat  Health aspects. I. Merzer, Glen. II. Title.
TX392.L94    1998
613.2'62–dc21    97-51961
CIP

ISBN 0-684-84516-4
0-684-85446-5 (Pbk)
For information regarding special discounts for bulk purchases,
please contact Simon & Schuster Special Sales at 1-800-456-6798
or business@simonandschuster.com

## ACKNOWLEDGMENTS

We would like to express our thanks to Charles Attwood, Ronnie Cummins, Richard DeAndrea, Reed and Prem Glidden, Michael Hansen, Susanne Havala, Matt and Mary Kelly, Michael Klaper, and John Stauber, for their advice, insight, and support. We are indebted as well to Gillian Blake for a brilliant job of editing, to Rick Rever and Steve Lustgarden for their suggestions, to Hans and Coby Seigenthaller for their endless hospitality, and to Marr Nealon and Patti Breitman for making this book possible. Erik Marcus deserves thanks not only for his thoughtful comments, but for writing the superb *Vegan: The New Ethics of Eating.* And we wish to acknowledge here gratefully an unsung hero of the environmental movement, Lynn Jacobs, whose extraordinary book, *Waste of the West: Public Lands Ranching,* is the most meticulous, carefully researched, comprehensively told story of what has happened to the ecology of the western United States. A special note of thanks as well to John Robbins, as generous a spirit as walks the earth. Finally, eternal gratitude to our wives, Willow Jeane Lyman and Joanna Samorow-Merzer, for putting up with us.

# CONTENTS

# Mad Cowboy

# CHAPTER ONE

# How to Tell the Truth and Get in Trouble

I am a fourth-generation dairy farmer and cattle rancher. I grew up on a dairy farm in Montana, and I ran a feedlot operation there for twenty years. I know firsthand how cattle are raised and how meat is produced in this country.

Today I am president of Earth Save International, an organization promoting organic farming and the vegitarian diet.

Sure, I used to enjoy my steaks as much as the next guy. But if you knew what I know about what goes into them and what they can do to you, you'd probably be a vegetarian like me. And, believe it or not, as a pure vegetarian now who consumes no animal products at all, I can tell you that these days I enjoy eating more than ever.

If you're a meat-eater in America, you have a right to know that you have something in common with most of the cows you've eaten. They've eaten meat, too.

When a cow is slaughtered, about half of it by weight is not eaten by humans: the intestines and their contents, the head, hooves, and horns, as well as bones and blood. These are dumped into giant grinders at rendering plants, as are the entire bodies of cows and other farm animals known to be diseased. Rendering is a $2.4-billion-a-year industry, processing forty billion pounds of dead animals a year. There is simply no such thing in America as an animal too ravaged by disease, too cancerous, or too putrid to be welcomed by the all-embracing arms of the renderer. Another staple of the renderer's diet, in addition to farm animals, is euthanized pets—the six or seven million dogs and cats that are killed in animal shelters every year. The city of Los Angeles alone, for example, sends some two hundred tons of euthanized cats and dogs to a rendering plant every month. Added to the blend are the euthanized catch of animal control agencies, and roadkill. (Roadkill is not collected daily, and in the summer, the better roadkill collection crews can generally smell it before they can see it.) When this gruesome mix is ground and steam-cooked, the lighter, fatty material floating to the top gets refined for use in such products as cosmetics, lubricants, soaps, candles, and waxes. The heavier protein material is dried and pulverized into a brown powder—about a quarter of which consists of fecal material. The powder is used as an additive to almost all pet food as well as to livestock feed. Farmers call it "protein concentrates." In 1995, five million tons of processed slaughterhouse leftovers were sold for animal feed in the United States. I used to feed tons of the stuff to my own livestock. It never concerned me that I was feeding cattle to cattle.

In August 1997, in response to growing concern about the spread of bovine spongiform encephalopathy (or Mad Cow disease), the FDA issued a new regulation that bans the feeding of ruminant protein (protein from cud-chewing animals) to ruminants; therefore, to the extent that the regulation is actually enforced, cattle are no longer quite the cannibals that we had made them into. They are no longer eating solid parts of other cattle, or sheep, or goats. They still munch, however, on ground-up dead horses, dogs, cats, pigs, chickens, and turkeys, as well as blood and fecal material of their own species and that of chickens. About 75 percent of the ninety million beef cattle in America are routinely given feed that has been "enriched" with rendered animal parts. The use of animal excrement in feed is common as well, as livestock operators have found it to be an efficient way of disposing of a portion of the 1.6 million tons of livestock wastes generated annually by their industry. In Arkansas, for example, the average farm feeds over fifty tons of chicken litter to cattle every year. One Arkansas cattle farmer was quoted in *U.S. News & World Report* as having recently purchased 745 tons of litter collected from the floors of local chicken-raising operations. After mixing it with small amounts of soybean bran, he then feeds it to his eight hundred head of cattle, making them, in his words, "fat as butterballs." He explained, "If I didn't have chicken litter, I'd have to sell half my herd. Other feeds are too expensive." If you are a meat-eater, understand that this is the food of your food.

We don't know all there is to know about the extent to which the consumption of diseased or unhealthy animals causes disease in humans, but we do know that some diseases—rabies, for example—are transmitted from the host animal to humans. We know that the common food poisonings brought on by such organisms as the prevalent E. coli bacteria, which results from fecal contamination of food, causes the death of nine thousand Americans a year and that about 80 percent of food poisonings come from tainted meat. And now we can also be certain, from the tragedy that has already afflicted Britain, that Mad Cow disease can "jump species" and give rise to a new variant of the always fatal, brain-wasting Creutzfeldt-Jakob disease in humans.

A funny thing can happen when you tell the truth in this country. You can get sued. In April of 1996, I was sitting on the stage of *The Oprah Winfrey Show,* looking into the shocked faces of a studio audience that was learning for the first time that we were turning cows into cannibals. "Right now," I explained, "we're following exactly the same path that they followed in England—ten years of dealing with [Mad Cow disease] as public relations rather than doing something substantial about it. A hundred thousand cows per year in the United States are fine one night, then [found] dead the following morning. The majority of those cows are . . . ground up and fed back to other cows. If only one of them has Mad Cow disease, it has the potential to affect thousands." Oprah herself was taken aback, and said quite simply, "Cows are herbivores. They shouldn't be eating other cows. . . . It has just stopped me cold from eating another burger."

Sitting next to me on the stage was a representative of the National Cattlemen's Beef Association, Dr. Gary Weber, whose job it was to reassure the viewing public of the absolute safety of meat. I felt sorry for the guy; he had an extremely difficult hand to play. He couldn't deny my assertion that we'd been feeding cows to cows, but belittling the fact didn't sit well with a gasping audience. During commercial breaks he privately agreed with me that we shouldn't be adding chopped-up cow to animal feed.

In early June, a suit was nonetheless filed on behalf of a group of Texas cattlemen, naming not only me but Oprah and her production company, Harpo Productions, as joint culprits in Food Disparagement. The Texas cattlemen and the Texas Commissioner of Agriculture apparently believe that the First Amendment to the Constitution of the United States, guar-

anteeing freedom of expression, was not meant to be inter-
preted so broadly as to allow people to say unpleasant things
about beef. Pointing to a drop in the cattle futures market, the
plaintiffs charged me with making "slanderous" statements
about cattle and beef that caused them to endure "shame, em-
barrassment, humiliation, and mental pain and anguish."
Under Texas's Food Disparagement law, the burden of proof
rests, to a great extent, on the shoulders of the defendants. In
January 1998, a jury was convened in Amarillo, Texas, to determine, among other things, whether my statements deviated
from "reasonable and reliable scientific inquiry, fact, or data"—
a standard of proof that seems remarkably oblivious of the fact
that disagreement has always existed within the scientific
community itself on most matters of importance, and certainly
exists now on the matter of Mad Cow disease. Controversy
even erupted in nineteenth-century Hungary when Dr. Ignaz
Philipp Semmelweis suggested that medical students delivering
babies should wash their hands first—especially as many of
them had come to the delivery room after dissecting corpses.
The man was roundly attacked for this radical view, but at least
he didn't have to face any Germ Disparagement laws.

Thirteen states have Food Disparagement laws on the
books. In Colorado, convicted food disparagers can even be
sent to jail. These laws represent the most concerted attack
on First Amendment freedoms in at least a generation, and
effectively put consumer advocates on notice that anything
they may have to say concerning the safety of any aspect of
our food supply could bring a bankrupting lawsuit smashing
down on their heads.

Oprah and I have the distinction of being the first individuals sued under the Texas Food Disparagement Act. More
than a year after we were sued, the second lawsuit premised

on the law was filed–by emu ranchers against the Honda Motor Company, whose television commercials they felt poked fun at emus. Emu prices had been plummeting for years, and I have a sneaking suspicion that the emu ranchers were secretly pleased to find an entity like Honda with deep pockets to blame it on. It seems that, in Texas at least, you can't be too careful what you say about cattle and emus.

Within a few months after the Oprah show aired and caused a firestorm of controversy, the Food and Drug Administration announced pending regulations to eliminate the feeding of ruminants to ruminants. The specific content of the regulations was delayed until after the presidential elections of 1996, most likely to avoid offending the livestock industry. Finally, the August 1997 ban on feeding ruminants to ruminants, a necessary but insufficient measure to stave off the spread of Mad Cow disease to America, went into effect.

Most of the media outlets in this country generate significant advertising revenues from the meat and dairy industries. After the Oprah show aired, I learned that the Beef Promotion Council pulled over six hundred thousand dollars' worth of network advertising. It's rare to find a media power player like Oprah, with the guts and the integrity to be willing to take on the big boys. I'll never forget that on the day of the show, Oprah told me privately that she had seen the movie *Babe* several times and would never eat pork again. During the show, she appeared to give up beef. Afterwards, I said, "Oprah, give me five minutes and I'll get you off chicken." She said, "One animal per day, please."

If you're going to be sued for disparaging beef, common sense alone would tell you to choose any setting other than Amarillo, Texas, for the site of the trial. Amarillo positively reeks of cows; the beef industry is a $3-billion-a-year industry there. Twenty-five percent of U.S. cattle are fattened in Amarillo feedlots before going to market. The town's biggest private employer is a slaughterhouse. A mural of cattle adorns the courthouse above the elevator. Amarillo is also the hometown of Paul Engler, a feedlot owner who was one of the plaintiffs in the lawsuit. An internal memo distributed by the president of the Amarillo Chamber of Commerce almost two weeks before the trial began reminded all concerned that the chamber "fully supports the cattle feed industry" and that there should be no "red carpet rollouts" for Oprah Winfrey. For all those reasons, our respective attorneys filed a pretrial motion asking that the trial be given a change of venue from Amarillo to the more neutral territory of Dallas. The motion was denied. My attorney took that as a legal setback, and an indication that the judge was hostile to our side, but I was secretly pleased. I liked the idea of giving my opponents their best shot. Let them have the hometown advantage, I thought. If Oprah and I prevailed, the victory would be all the sweeter.

Oprah could have easily afforded to pay the millions of dollars she was being sued for, but to her credit she fought both for her reputation and for freedom of speech, and moved her television show from Chicago to Amarillo for the trial. Reporters followed her like flies to a feedlot. Neither she nor I could step up to the microphones, however, as Judge Mary Lou Robinson had imposed a gag order on all parties for the duration of the trial. Day after day on the news, Oprah could be seen shrugging in uncharacteristic muteness at the cameras as she entered and left the courthouse. For some reason, the press showed less interest in me, and I can state unequivocally that absolutely no member of the press whatsoever showed any interest at all in what I was wearing.

I was on the witness stand for two days. Since the Food Disparagement law on which the plaintiffs' case was premised makes a person liable if he or she knowingly gives information that "states or implies" that a "perishable food product is not safe for consumption by the public," and that information is judged to be false according to "reasonable and reliable scientific inquiry, facts, or data," the plaintiffs' attorney had to first establish that I had disseminated certain "facts." He would then have to prove that those facts were "false," and that I had known they were false. But I simply denied that my warnings of the dangers of Mad Cow disease spreading to the States were "facts" at all. I repeatedly said I was expressing only my opinion. And while I firmly believe that my warning that the practice of cow cannibalism could have tragic consequences falls into the category of "opinion" rather than "fact"—how, after all, can there be a fact about the future?—the idea that millions of dollars' worth of liability should rest on such distinctions endangers healthy debate in a free society. The exercise I went through on the stand simply has no place in the America that I believe in. I had to answer questions such as, "Has anyone ever said you were irresponsible?" I was under oath, in a court of law. I couldn't lie. "My wife," I said.

When Oprah took the stand, she called the lawsuit "the most painful thing I've ever experienced." Then she added, "I feel in my heart I've never done a malicious act against any human being." I believe her. Throughout the trial, inside and outside the courtroom, I never heard her say an unkind word about anyone, even the cattlemen who had attacked her reputation for integrity. "I just don't understand why I'm here," she often said. As she pointed out on the stand, she had invited two guests on the show to present the beef industry's point of view. She had even allowed one of them, Dr. Weber, to return for a follow-up show, without me or any other food safety activist present to counter his claims. Oprah could hardly be fairly accused of harboring an anti-beef agenda, and yet here she was in Amarillo, accused of just that.

Mr. Engler, our accuser, took the stand and testified that he might not have filed suit if I had qualified my statements on the air as simply my opinions. He said that Dr. Weber was not under any such obligation to qualify his statements because he had more credibility by virtue of having a Ph.D. and not being a vegetarian. My attorney pointed out that Engler and I had some things in common: both of us have bachelor's degrees in agriculture, and both of us became cattlemen who once sold off our cattle to cover debts. Therefore, my attorney asked, "If you appeared on a national talk show, would you have to say that you were expressing an opinion?"

"No," Engler answered.

"Is the main difference between you and Mr. Lyman that you don't agree with him?" my attorney asked.

"No, sir. It's difficult to say," Engler said. He paused, then explained, "Mr. Lyman's a liar."

The jury didn't buy his logic. On February 26, 1998, the long ordeal came to an end when the jury, after a deliberation that lasted less than six hours, found us not liable for damages. It was a wonderful day for me, full of the joy that comes of relief from torment. But there are better kinds of joy, and I wouldn't wish the experience of a potentially bankrupting lawsuit on my worst enemy. I hope that the thirteen states that currently have food libel laws, and the fourteen other states that are reported to be currently considering enacting them, note that the trial became something of a bad joke throughout the nation. And I hope and trust that these laws will soon be found unconstitutional.

I can tell you as a former Alleged Food Disparager that behind the absurdity of this lawsuit lay an ugly reality. The

American people have been raised to believe that someone is looking out for their food safety. The disturbing truth is that the protection of the quality of our food is the mandate of foot-dragging bureaucrats at the U.S. Department of Agriculture and the Food and Drug Administration who can generally be counted upon to behave not like public servants but like hired hands of the meat and dairy industries.

My journey from feedlot operator to cattlemen's nemesis has been a strange ride, one that has brought me from castrating calves to experiencing the frustrations of Washington politics, from embracing high-tech agriculture to getting sued by its practitioners. I don't pretend to understand the meaning of every bump in the road I've traveled. Hell, I sometimes feel like I was unconscious for the first half of the trip. But I can say this much for sure: all the signposts along the way concerned my health. Every time I instinctively made a choice consistent with the improvement of my physical health, it was as if more light was shed to guide me on what has turned out to be a marvelous path.

In writing this book, it is my purpose, more than anything else, to share what I've learned about how the best choices for our personal health turn out to be the best choices for the world we inhabit.

For all too many Americans, the first decision they consciously make about their health is the stark one between bypass surgery and angioplasty, or between chemotherapy and radiation. In reality, however, we knowingly or unknowingly make choices every day that can either lead us toward those grim options, or else toward happier ones. We do so, of course, every time we decide what fuel to put in our bodies.

To make our choices informed ones, we have to start with the facts.

CHAPTER TWO

# The Simple Facts

There are only two things wrong with meat: what we know for sure is in it, and all the other stuff that might be in it.

Nearly all meat in America is contaminated with such man-made carcinogens as dioxins, a family of chemicals related to Agent Orange, and DDT, the notorious chemical that was banned domestically over twenty-five years ago but that remains in the ground (and will remain there, unfortunately, for thousands of years to come) and therefore in the crops fed to animals. Crops grown for cattle feed are permitted to, and almost always do, contain far higher levels of pesticides than crops grown for human consumption. About 80 percent of pesticides used in America are targeted on four specific crops—corn, soybeans, cotton, and wheat—that are the major constituents of livestock feed. Since animals store pesticides and other toxic substances in their fat, they get their most concentrated doses of these carcinogens when they eat other animals. And we in turn get even more concentrated doses of carcinogens when we eat them.

According to a 1975 study by the Council on Environmental Quality, 95 percent of the human intake of DDT came from dairy and meat products. When we don't eat animal products, we can largely avoid pesticide residues. A study published in the *New England Journal of Medicine* found that the breast milk of vegetarian women had only *1 to 2 percent* of the national average of pesticide contamination.

Of course, there are many carcinogens in our environment, and there is often a lag of ten or twenty or even thirty years before a cancer-causing agent produces the full-blown tumor that can kill a person, so it is always difficult to attribute any given cancer to a particular source with anything approaching scientific certainty. But we do know that the incidence of cancer in the human population, and most notably in industrialized societies, has skyrocketed during this century, and the increase continues unabated. When President Nixon declared a national War on Cancer in 1971, about one in five Americans could expect to be afflicted with cancer in their lifetimes. Today, that figure is one in three. Many studies have implicated pesticides as a major source of cancer risk. The evidence mounts that farmers, who have greater contact with pesticides than the general population, are suffering a disproportionate incidence of cancer. As we go down the mine of chemical agriculture, our farmers may unfortunately be serving as our canaries.

But there is a difference between established scientific fact and speculation, even when that speculation centers on matters as troubling as the feeding of animal parts and feces to the nation's livestock, and the hemisphere-sized experiment, just thirty years old, of the prolific use of pesticides, in which humans as well as farm animals have been the unwitting guinea pigs.

So let us set aside speculation for the moment and begin simply from one indisputable scientific fact about flesh consumption: meat kills. It kills us just as dead as tobacco kills us, but far more frequently. It is far and away the number-one cause of death and disease in America. One out of every two Americans alive today will die of cardiovascular disease, usually in the form of a heart attack. And heart attacks are never caused by corn, broccoli, or cauliflower; they are not the work of pears, plums, or peaches; they are never brought on by rice, barley, or lentils. They can virtually always be attributed to saturated fat and cholesterol. Since saturated fat is converted by the liver into cholesterol, these two agents work hand in hand. In excess, they begin clogging our arteries, causing atherosclerosis, the major factor in heart disease. Although it's certainly possible to get too much fat from a select few plant-based foods (oils, margarine, nuts, seeds, and avocados, for example), most of the saturated fat in the standard American diet and *all* the cholesterol come from animal products. Study after study has linked the consumption of animal products to heart disease. When I say to you that the consumption of meat, fish, poultry, and dairy products is the primary cause of atherosclerosis in nonsmokers (for smokers, cigarettes may be equally to blame), I am not just giving my opinion; I am reporting a medical fact that has been established with as much scientific unanimity and consistency as the fact that smoking cigarettes dramatically increases the risk of lung cancer, emphysema, and heart disease. But it is a fact that simply hasn't yet been established as firmly in the public mind, thanks in large part to the obfuscations of the meat and dairy industries, which have taken a lesson from the tobacco industry in how to stay in business while killing people. Their policy is simple: deny, and when you can't deny, confuse. One of the most effective means of confusion has been to imply to the American people that heart disease is a "natural cause" of death. But as the noted preventive health care expert Dr. Julian Whitaker points out, "Death of heart disease is as unnecessary as dying of drug abuse, yet it is taken as a normal thing."

When atherosclerosis sets in, one of two things usually happens. Either the coronary arteries get clogged, cutting off the supply of blood to the heart, and a heart attack ensues; or the arteries feeding the brain get clogged, cutting off the supply of blood to the brain, and a stroke ensues. Thus animal products in our diet are the primary culprits not only in heart attacks but in strokes as well.

Stress is an aggravating factor, too, of course, and scientific evidence has accumulated that loneliness, or a sense of emotional isolation, adds substantially to an individual's risk of heart trouble. So you may well reap a windfall of health benefits if you can find ways to reduce stress in your life and develop or enhance intimate relationships with others. But few people are lucky enough to escape periods of stress, loneliness, or loss altogether, and given a choice, I'd rather undergo these hardships with a healthy set of arteries than with arteries clogged by saturated fats and cholesterol. A study of mortality following a major earthquake in Athens, Greece, in 1981 strongly indicated that "stress-related sudden cardiac deaths tend to occur in a background of athero-sclerotic disease." Dr. Dean Ornish, who has done pioneering work on reversing heart disease, explains the physiological basis for this reality:

*Recent research shows that the lining of normal coronary arteries produces a substance called endothelium-derived relaxation factor, or EDRF, that dilates the coronary arteries, allowing more*

*blood to flow to the heart. When the lining of the coronary ar-*
*teries is damaged by atherosclerosis, much less EDRF is pro-*
*duced, so the arteries tend to restrict and reduce coronary*
*blood flow. As a result, atherosclerotic arteries tend to be hy-*
*perresponsive to stress.*

If stress itself were really a leading cause of heart attacks, surely the number of heart attacks would have risen dramatically in Europe during World War II. But in fact the death rate from heart disease fell, as people in war-ravaged countries were forced by circumstance to eat less rich, high-fat, cholesterol-laden foods. In other words, it's demonstrably better for your heart to eat a low-fat, vegetarian diet while bombs drop all around you than to enjoy your steak in peace.

Now if I were to tell you that tobacco is an evil weed and that we have to do all we can to stop our young people from getting addicted to those nicotine delivery systems known as cigarettes, you probably wouldn't blink an eye. But if I were to tell you that animal products in our diet are an at least equivalent evil, and that we have to do all we can to keep our young people from getting hooked on those fat-and-cholesterol delivery systems known as hot dogs, hamburgers, scrambled eggs, and ice cream, you might think I'd gone a little over the edge.

But the evidence that animal products are our number-one killer is hard to dispute. Here are just some of the studies that, beginning a generation ago, have established this fact:

*A study in 1970 analyzed the relationship between dietary*
*intake of saturated fat and cholesterol and heart disease in*

*12,000 men in seven countries, including the United States. It found the highest rate of death from heart disease in the two countries with the highest consumption of saturated fat and cholesterol—Finland and the United States.*

*An extraordinary study conducted in the mid-1970's of no less than 24,000 Seventh-Day Adventists—whose diet is higher than the American norm in whole grains, fruits, and vegetables, and lower in animal products—compared meat-eaters to both lacto-ovo vegetarians (who consume milk and eggs) and vegans (pure vegetarians who consume no animal products at all). It found the rate of heart disease mortality to be one-third as high for the lacto-ovo vegetarians as for the meat-eaters. For the vegans, the rate was one-tenth as high.*

*A study published in 1988 of close to five thousand British vegetarians found the death rate from heart disease of male vegetarians to be 44% of that of the general population; for female vegetarians, the comparable figure was 41%.*

*A massive population study known as the China Health Project has determined that those who eat the least animal products have the lowest rates of cancer, heart disease, and several other degenerative diseases.*

*A study in Germany tracking more than 1,900 vegetarians for eleven years found their death rate to be about half that of the rest of the population. There were less than one-half the expected deaths from cardiovascular disease in both sexes and low rates for cancers of the digestive tract. The subjects of the study were generally "moderate" lacto-ovo vegetarians, not vegans.*

*In the United States, lacto-ovo vegetarians have cholesterol levels that are 14% lower than meat-eaters', and vegans have cholesterol levels (averaging 128) that are 35% lower!*

Even as early as 1961, believe it or not, the *Journal of the American Medical Association* announced: "A vegetarian diet can prevent 97% of our coronary occlusions." Over the succeeding decades, as the evidence of the link between dietary cholesterol and heart disease mounted, the general public responded. Many people are now concerned with their cholesterol levels and take their doctors' advice to eat less red meat and cut down on eggs, often in the hope of getting their cholesterol down to the "normal" 200 level. And they often try to watch their intake of fat. Since close to 40 percent of the caloric intake of the standard American diet comes in the form of fat, many people try to eat "lean" meats, frequently replacing red meat with fish and chicken, and to cut down on fried food in order to reduce their fat intake to the 30 percent level recommended (as an upper limit) by the American Heart Association. And then, with appalling frequency, they still get heart disease and wonder what they did wrong.

What they did wrong was to start from a diet that is profoundly counterproductive to human health, and then make modest improvements. This approach might be compared to wearing a parka in Death Valley in July, then starting to worry about heat prostration, and opening a button or two. The truth is that a cholesterol level of around 200 can be labeled "normal" only in the sense that getting a heart attack in America is "normal." A truly heart-healthy cholesterol level is 150 or below. Since 1948, 5,209 residents of Framingham, Massachusetts, have been studied by researchers looking for risk factors of coronary heart disease. The good news is that, in all that time, they have not found a single person to have a heart attack whose blood cholesterol was less than 150! The bad news is that, unless your serum cholesterol is under or near that 150 level, you may never know if heart disease is creeping up on you. The Framingham study showed that, ". . . among persons examined less than 2 years before their death, 94% of those destined to die of heart disease before age 65 either had no heart disease . . . or had only a mild form of heart disease." The researchers aptly called it "a disease which can be silent even in its most dangerous form."

Most people cannot get their cholesterol to that magical 150 level by making minor changes in a meat-based diet. A study in Italy in 1980 of 127 subjects put on a "low-fat" (25 percent of caloric intake as fat) diet containing meat resulted in a lowering of the participants' average cholesterol levels by only a statistically insignificant 2.8 percent after four weeks. Then one single change was made. The meat in the diet was replaced with a textured soybean product called TVP. Two weeks later, average cholesterol levels were down almost 20 percent. After two more weeks on the TVP, the total cholesterol drop was about 25 percent. No subject failed to achieve a cholesterol drop of at least 10 percent. Clearly, the only dependable, nonpharmaceutical route to a significant drop in blood cholesterol is to move to a plant-based diet.

No other factor rivals diet as a cause of atherosclerosis. There is a myth circulating in the land that our genes play a leading role in determining our risk of a heart attack. The truth is, there's only one thing we're likely to inherit that can cause a heart attack, and that's bad eating habits. While some people may have a genetic disposition to elevated cholesterol that can aggravate the damage caused by a meat-based diet, virtually none of us would need to worry about any danger of a heart attack if we abstained from animal foods. As Dr. Whitaker explains, "For some reason there is widespread belief that heart disease is an inherited disease, with family history playing the strong role in who is to suffer and die from it. In reality, heart disease is a nutritional disease for the overwhelming majority, and family history has little to do with it."

In Japan, heart disease is much less prevalent than in America, yet when Japanese people live in the United States and adopt the American diet, their rate of heart disease increases as much as tenfold—a clear indication that diet, not heredity, reigns as the determining factor in heart disease. For those who have been persuaded that they suffer from an inherited tendency to heart disease, the natural reactions may include anger, fear, self-loathing, and, perhaps most damaging of all, a sense of helplessness. Here's the good news for the people who suffer from this notion: you are almost undoubtedly not fated to perish of heart disease. You have control of the most important factor in heart disease—your diet.

Just as some people wrongly believe that they are condemned to heart disease by bad genes, others are so certain that their health is protected by good genes that they don't worry about the ill effects of eating high-cholesterol foods. It's true that some people have a genetic predisposition to low blood cholesterol levels, probably because they excrete cholesterol more efficiently than most people. But listen to what Dr. John McDougall, who grew up on the standard American diet, suffered a stroke at the age of eighteen, and has now become a leading dietary researcher and proponent of vegetarian living, has to say about those rare individuals who eat animal-based diets and still boast low cholesterol levels:

> ... *Even though these people will have a lower risk of heart disease, they still have health risks from consuming so much cholesterol.*
>
> *Excreted cholesterol enters the gallbladder and thereby contributes to the production of gallstones (90 percent of gallstones are made of cholesterol) and excessive amounts of cholesterol in the lower intestines are believed to be involved in the development of colon cancer. Vegetable oils will cause cholesterol to be eliminated from the body, lowering our risk of heart disease. Unfortunately, however, because this cholesterol is excreted through the gallbladder and into the colon, your risks of developing gallbladder disease and colon cancer are increased the more cholesterol you excrete. Thus, a change to a no-cholesterol diet is not only the most effective, but the safest way to lower your cholesterol level.*

Dr. Ornish has found that it is possible to reverse the course of coronary disease with a truly low-fat (10 percent fat) plant-based diet. The only animal products allowed on his diet are nonfat milk, nonfat yogurt, and egg whites. When he instructed his patients to combine this diet with a lifestyle program described in his book *Dr. Dean Ornish's Program for Reversing Heart Disease*, the following results were obtained:

> *After only one year, the majority (82 percent) of the patients who made the comprehensive lifestyle changes . . . demonstrated some measurable average reversal of their coronary*

*artery blockages. . . . Overall, the average blockage reversed from 61.1 to 55.8 percent; more severely blocked arteries showed even greater improvement.*

There is no technological quick fix for the damage done to arteries by years of eating fatty and cholesterol-laden foods. The medical profession nonetheless often recommends heart bypass surgery, a traumatic form of intervention that is always risky and often causes more harm than good. A major study of 780 heart patients, half treated with surgery and half with medication, concluded that longevity rates were not improved by surgery. And yet, due to the distressing effects of the use of the heart-lung machine during bypass surgery, damage can occur to many of the body's vital organs, particularly the brain, which, according to several studies, is at least somewhat injured in all bypass operations.

Not only is a vegetarian diet the best preventive medicine for our hearts, it may also help us begin finally to win a war we've been losing since it's been declared: the war on cancer.

The German Cancer Research Center conducted a study of over 1,900 vegetarians, and found that rates for all forms of cancer were only 56 percent of the normal rate. The aforementioned study of Seventh-Day Adventist men also found that this group, about half of whom are vegetarian, and who eat on average about 50 percent more fiber than the general population, suffers 55 percent less prostate cancer than other American males. Similarly, a ten-year study of over 120,000 Japanese men reported that vegetarian men had a lower incidence of prostate cancer than meat-eaters. This study may have been both confirmed and explained by a recent British study of 696 men that found vegan men to have lower levels of insulin-like growth factor, of IGF-I, than meat-eaters. IGF-I has been implicated in causing prostate cancer.

An investigation by the National Cancer Institute correlated the incidence of colon cancer with over a hundred specific foods. All types of dead animals fared the worst. "Risks of beef, pork, and chicken all rose with frequency of use, and the composite picture suggests an underlying dose-response relationship." The Association for the Advancement of Science reported: "Populations on a high-meat, high-fat diet are more likely to develop colon cancer than individuals on vegetarian or similar low-meat diets." And in 1991, a thirty-six-country study reported a strong and direct correlation between consumption of dairy and animal fat and the incidence of prostate cancer, colorectal cancer, lung cancer, and breast cancer.

Worldwide epidemiological evidence also reveals a remarkably direct link between dietary fat intake and breast cancer deaths. Nations like Thailand and El Salvador with a comparatively low-fat, plant-based diet have the lowest breast cancer mortality rates. The highest rates are in the "high-fat" countries like the Netherlands, the United Kingdom, Denmark, Canada, New Zealand, Switzerland, and the United States.

Lest anyone think that demographic comparisons of cancer rates can be better explained by genetics than patterns of food consumption, consider that as Japan has Westernized over the last thirty years, dramatically increasing the percentage of fat and dairy products in its diet, the rate of breast cancer in that country has shot up in an equally dramatic way. A massive Japanese study documented a breast cancer risk in daily meat-eaters that was four times the risk of those who ate little or no meat. Breast cancer rates also varied directly with consumption of eggs, butter, and cheese. Not surprisingly, in the United States, Seventh-Day Adventist women have markedly lower rates of cervical and ovarian cancer than the rest of the population. A 1989 Harvard study also linked dairy consumption directly with ovarian cancer.

Finally, the less-than-radical National Academy of Sciences came to the following verdict in 1982: "In summary, the incidence of prostate cancer is correlated with other cancers associated with diet, e.g., breast cancer. There is good evidence that an increased risk of prostate cancer is associated with certain dietary factors, especially the intake of high fat and high protein foods, which usually occur together in the diet. There is some evidence that foods rich in Vitamin A . . . and vegetarian diets are associated with a lower risk."

In short, the evidence that an animal-based diet is implicated in our soaring cancer rates—our number-two killer—begins to rival the evidence of its contribution to our number-one killer, coronary heart disease.

When meat and dairy products aren't killing us, they're often making us sick and progressively destroying our health and the quality of our lives. We are one of the most obese nations on Earth, and as a result have created a diet industry that generates $40 billion annually. But in China, where the average person consumes, believe it or not, 25 percent *more* calories daily than in the United States, obesity is extremely rare. The difference is that the Chinese consume a plant-based diet, far lower in fat than the standard American diet. It's that simple. Know anyone who got fat on rice?

Osteoporosis ranks as one of the great scourges of our senior citizens, contributing to crippling bone fractures in millions of Americans. We've all heard about osteoporosis: it's caused by a lack of calcium in the diet, and the best way to combat it is by drinking a lot of calcium-rich milk, right? Wrong. While the dairy industry tries hard to promote the idea that milk fights osteoporosis, they cannot make it come true. Osteoporosis is yet another disease of the animal-based diet, and the consumption of milk and meat—both calcium-rich—is nonetheless more likely to aggravate the condition than to mitigate it. Again, comparing cultures with different diets overwhelmingly proves the case. The Chinese, who eat almost no dairy, get all their calcium from plant sources and consume only 6 percent of the animal protein of the average American, rarely suffer from osteoporosis. The Eskimos, while not milk-drinkers, do eat a calcium-rich diet of meat and fish, and have an astoundingly high rate of osteoporosis.

A study of 1,600 women compared bone loss in vegetarians with bone loss in meat-eaters. It found that by the time they reached eighty, vegetarian women had lost only about half as much bone mineral as meat-eaters. Since the human body cannot store excess protein, it excretes it through the urine, taking calcium with it. Excess proteins cause an acid load in the blood; in order to neutralize this load, calcium is depleted from the bones. The dairy industry won't be the first to tell you this, but the dietary cause of osteoporosis is rarely a deficiency of calcium; it is instead a surfeit of protein, the natural result of an animal-based diet. This surfeit of protein, in addition to stressing the kidneys, results in the loss of bone density that we call osteoporosis. While milk contains calcium, it also contains so much protein that it winds up costing the body more of the mineral than it adds. If you want to avoid osteoporosis, the best prescription is a simple one: get your calcium from any of a variety of calcium-rich vegetarian foods—almonds, sesame seeds, molasses, garbanzo beans, tofu (made with calcium sulfate), broccoli, and kale, for example—and keep your protein intake reasonably low, to about 10 to 20 percent of caloric intake. And tune out the propaganda of the dairy industry.

Diabetes is yet another affliction that is in some cases caused by, in other cases aggravated by, a meat-based diet. Compared with the general population, Seventh-Day Adventists have roughly half the risk of developing diabetes. A study of diabetics showed that those placed on a high-fiber vegetarian diet required 73 percent less insulin therapy than those on standard diets. Diabetics often need insulin shots not because their bodies don't produce enough insulin (they in fact do) but because the insulin they produce fails to function at least partially as a result of high levels of fat in the blood. A low-fat, high-fiber diet can do more to help most diabetics than insulin pumps and medication. As the vegetarian author and health expert John Robbins points out, diabetes "is rare or nonexistent among peoples whose diets are primarily grains, vegetables, and fruits. If these same people switch to rich meat-based diets, however, their incidence of diabetes balloons."

Hypertension, or high blood pressure, is a complicating factor in both cardiovascular and cerebrovascular disease. It is the most common reason for a visit to the doctor in America, and more prescriptions are written for hypertension than for any other disease. It is almost axiomatic in our country that as one grows older, one's blood pressure rises, and as a result one is at greater risk of a stroke or a heart attack. This is not because the human body was designed to self-destruct this way, but because an animal-based diet high in saturated fats and cholesterol narrows our arteries, thus increasing the pressure of the blood flowing through them. When such a condition leads to a fatal heart attack or stroke in an older person, we often say the person "died of old age." It would be more accurate to say that the victim "died of the American diet."

Scientific studies have implicated meat again and again as a cause of high blood pressure, revealing the vegetarian diet as the optimal long-term solution. One study published more than twenty years ago in the *New England Journal of Medicine* compared 115 vegetarians to the same number of meat-eaters. The systolic blood pressure (measured as the heart contracts) of the vegetarians was 9.3 percent lower than the meat-eaters'; the diastolic blood pressure (measured as the heart relaxes) 18.2 percent lower. Dozens of studies have demonstrated similar results—the first of which was a particularly cruel one conducted in 1926 that showed a significant rise in the blood pressure of vegetarians fed meat!

The benefits of a low-fat vegetarian diet also include reduced risk of hypoglycemia, ulcers, intestinal disorders, gout and other forms of arthritis, kidney stones, gallstones, asthma, impotence, and, believe it or not, even anemia. Despite myths to the contrary, a well-balanced vegetarian diet without dairy products will generally be higher in iron than a meat-based diet. Unfortunately, since many lacto-vegetarians (particularly women) eat a lot of dairy out of a misguided fear that they won't get enough protein otherwise, they run the risk of anemia only because dairy products are deficient in iron.

Many people concerned about the health risks of a meat-based diet have adopted the half-measure of cutting down on red meat and eating more chicken and fish. Some people who consume fish and poultry while avoiding red meat entirely even call themselves "semi-vegetarian." Unfortunately for them, chicken and fish are not plants, and they are not health foods. It is not even clear that they are lesser evils than red meat. Only modern linguistic convention saves fish and poultry from the label of "meat"—for they are indeed meats, the flesh of animals. Substituting chicken and fish for red meat will not help you avoid any of the health risks associated with the meat of mammals. It will not save you from heart disease, strokes, diabetes, cancer, high blood pressure, or osteoporosis. Chicken and fish will in fact contribute to the danger of developing those conditions. They present the exact same threats to our well-being as red meat: they are high in fat (especially saturated fat), high in cholesterol, too high in protein, high in pesticide residue, and devoid of fiber and complex carbohydrates. There is a popular misconception that chicken and fish are low-cholesterol foods, or at least considerably lower than beef. A 3.5-ounce serving of beef contains 85 milligrams of cholesterol. The same-size serving of chicken (white meat, skinned) also has 85 milligrams of cholesterol. With equivalent servings of pork, trout, and turkey, you can clog your arteries with 90, 73, and 82 milligrams of cholesterol, respectively. There simply are no low-cholesterol flesh foods, and there are no plant foods with any cholesterol.

More than 90 percent of chickens are raised on factory

farms where they typically dine very cheaply—on their own fecal material. It is not surprising, therefore, that a recent Agriculture Department study revealed that more than 99 percent of broiler carcasses had dectectable levels of E. coli. In addition, approximately 30 percent of chicken consumed in America is contaminated with salmonella, and 70 to 90 percent with another deadly pathogen, campylobacter. While it doesn't share the notoriety of salmonella (probably because it's more difficult to pronounce and spell), campylobacter causes two hundred to eight hundred deaths a year, as well as two to eight million cases a year of a sickness, campylobacteriosis, whose symptoms can include cramps, abdominal pain, bloody diarrhea, and fever. The pathogen also brings on perhaps as many as two thousand cases per year of a rare paralytic disease, Guillain-Barré syndrome, whose victims are usually required to stay for a period of weeks in the intensive care unit hooked up to a respirator. The bacterium has proved increasingly resistant to the antibiotics that would normally be used to treat its human victims, as drug-resistant strains have evolved from the use of antibiotics to fight disease in chickens.

Slaughterhouses are efficient factories for spreading pathogens from one chicken to the next. According to the independent Government Accountability Project, up to 25 percent of chickens on the inspection line are covered with feces, bile, and feed, and chickens are often soaked in chlorine baths to remove slime and odor. You will be reassured to know that, in order to protect your health, individual chicken inspectors examine about twelve thousand chickens a day, each for about two seconds. In spite of those two-second inspections, contaminated chicken still manages to kill at least one thousand Americans a year, and estimates of how many they sicken range as high as 80 million.

By rights, bacteria ought to be able to call themselves "semi-vegetarian," because in addition to chicken, they seem to love fish. If their goal is to reach humans, they've made a wise choice: fish is not generally inspected even to the paltry degree that beef and poultry are. A thorough 1992 *Consumer Reports* study on the safety of the fish Americans eat found nearly half the fish tested contaminated by bacteria from human or animal feces. The Centers for Disease Control reports conservatively 325,000 cases of food poisoning annually in this country from contaminated seafood. Fish are generally considered to begin to spoil when bacteria grow to between one and ten million colonies per gram. Sampling fish from markets in the New York, Chicago, and Santa Cruz/San Jose metropolitan areas, *Consumer Reports* found almost 40 percent of the fish tested in the "beginning to spoil" range, and an additional 25 percent of the samples with bacterial counts that "exceeded the upper limits of our test method," meaning they had more than 27 million colonies per gram. Often, fish that reach your dinner table have been dead for two weeks or more, and the bacteria that live on them generally have no problem thriving in your refrigerator. To add insult to injury, you often can't be sure what type of fish you're really eating: upwards of 30 percent of fish were found in the same study to be mislabeled. Thawed fish are often labeled "fresh," and many fish magically change species on their journey from the sea to the kitchen.

Fish is sometimes touted for possessing omega-3 fatty acid, but this nutrient can just as easily be obtained by consuming soy products, pumpkin and flax seeds, canola and walnut oils, dark green vegetables, and wheat germ. What fish *does* have that those other foods don't are high cholesterol content and a wide assortment of such chemical toxins as mercury, lead, pesticides, and PCBs. The municipal wastes and agricultural chemicals that we flush into our waters become absorbed in the tissues of fish and shellfish and thus into most of the items on the menu at your favorite seafood restaurant. The *Consumer Reports* study found PCBs in 43 percent of salmon and 25 percent of swordfish. Catfish had significant levels of DDT, clams had high levels of lead, and 90 percent of swordfish contained mercury. The study concluded that for "pregnant women or women who expect to become pregnant, there's little choice but to avoid many popular types of fish. Salmon, swordfish, and lake whitefish may well contain polychlorinated biphenyls . . . which can accumulate in the body to the point where they pose a risk to the developing fetus." Evidence for this warning comes from women who ate fish from Lake Michigan containing PCBs: a study showed that they gave birth to smaller-than-average babies with significant developmental problems.

In sum, fish and chicken are not truly alternatives to red meat; they are best thought of as merely different types of flesh foods sharing some of the same drawbacks as any meat (high fat, high cholesterol, no fiber), as well as presenting some dangers uniquely their own.

Earlier I compared meat to tobacco as a killer, but to be fair, in one way alone tobacco outshines meat as an evil: it is physically addictive. As we all know, tobacco companies have a history of trying to target their ads to teenagers in the frequently fulfilled hope that these young people will be in their thrall for the rest of their lives. Meat, by contrast, is in no way physically addictive. Eating it is merely a habit, one that people are socially conditioned to believe is normal, even healthy. Whether you choose to phase meat out of your diet slowly, over time, or to stop on a dime and become a vegetarian overnight, you won't suffer any real symptoms of "withdrawal." But you probably *will* feel more energy, and enjoy a longer and healthier life. The damage already done to your arteries by saturated fat and cholesterol may well reverse. By dramatically reducing your intake of animal products, or better yet by becoming a pure vegetarian, you can effectively begin to cleanse your arteries. In the process, you are likely to avoid not only heart disease and strokes but also such diverse ailments as high blood pressure, diabetes, osteoporosis, and certain types of cancer. In a sense, all these different problems are really just varied symptoms of a disease called the animal-based diet.

Although ours will probably never become a vegetarian nation, nor a vegetarian planet, it will soon have to become a *more vegetarian* nation and a *more vegetarian* planet—by which I mean both that there will be a greater percentage of pure vegetarians in the population and that those who remain omnivores will eat far less meat than they do now—or else we're going to see starvation and death on a scale unparalleled in human history, within the lifetime of the young people of today.

The reasons for these assertions are simple. As Frances Moore Lappé first pointed out to the general public in *Diet for a Small Planet,* producing beef is an extraordinarily inefficient business. It takes sixteen pounds of grain to create one pound of beef. If a subsistence daily ration of grain is about a half pound, then the same amount of grain needed to produce one pound of meat could feed thirty-two people a day if they ate the grain directly. And so as our population increases, we will basically face the choice of whether to continue feeding our corn, wheat, barley, oats, and soybeans to animals, while letting untold millions go hungry, or else to eat our grains directly, and have many times as much food available for human consumption. In feeding grain to cattle, we forfeit 90 percent of the original protein, 99 percent of the carbohydrates, and 100 percent of the fiber. When you consider that an acre of fertile land can produce forty thousand pounds of potatoes, thirty thousand pounds of carrots, fifty thousand pounds of tomatoes, or two hundred fifty pounds of beef, you begin to get an idea of the inherent inefficiency of raising meat.

If you think that we are currently using our agricultural surplus to feed the hungry world, consider that two-thirds of our agricultural exports go to feed livestock abroad. We are helping to fatten animals for slaughter everywhere. It is generally only people who are left hungry.

Barring some horrific war or catastrophic outbreak of disease, the current population of the earth—over six billion people—will roughly double within the next sixty years. There will likely be ten to twelve billion people sharing this planet by the year 2060. By far the greater share of that population growth will take place in countries that are already relatively poor and hungry. A recent report of the Worldwatch Institute indicated that in 1994, for the first time, there were more people on the planet than could adequately be fed by our usage of the food supply, even if global food distribution systems were optimal—and of course they remain far from optimal. We are now annually losing ground in the global war on hunger and the struggle for food security.

The twin horns of the dilemma are population growth

and grain usage. (Actually, there is what we might call a third horn, elucidated by Lappé and Joseph Collins in *Food First*, and that is the hijacking of agricultural systems in hungry countries for the purpose of growing lucrative export crops. Much of that abuse takes the form of the raising of beef for consumption in richer countries.) In both the developed and the developing worlds, an increasing percentage of grain is now being diverted to animal feed. Meanwhile, over the last few years, as population pressures have advanced unabated, global grain production has leveled off. As the planet becomes more populated, greater and greater stress is put on the land, and acreage once devoted to agriculture is developed for housing or transportation or industry. If, for example, development continues at the current pace in the marvelously fertile Central Valley of California, arguably the richest agricultural prize in the world, a million acres of farmland will be lost by the year 2040. It's estimated that, by the year 2080, the valley won't even be able to feed itself, much less continue to produce a harvest of two hundred fifty crops currently worth $13 billion. In China, should population growth and food utilization patterns continue uninterrupted, by the year 2030 that nation will need to import twice as much grain as is currently exported today *from all countries to all countries*. And by that time, China will have been surpassed in population by India. In short, there's no way in hell that we're ever going to be able to feed ten to twelve billion people on this planet if we keep diverting even the percentage we now divert—much less an *increasing* percentage—of our grain to animals.

But the Council on Agricultural Science and Technology gives us a more hopeful perspective. The think tank says that we could manage to feed ten billion people with the available crop land we have today, using current technology—*with the single proviso that the population of the world becomes vegetarian.*

The seas do not provide us with an alternative; instead, their condition makes the outlook for the food supply appear more stark. Humanity's appetite for fish has long since outstripped the resources of the sea. All of the world's major fishing grounds have been stressed to their limits. Sophisticated fishing vessels deploying fishing nets wide enough to haul in a dozen 747 jumbo jets have not only taken the sport out of fishing, they have depleted our oceans and pushed many individual species to the brink of extinction. Two of the world's most productive fishing areas, Canada's Grand Banks and New England's Georges Bank, are considered commercially extinct. In 1994, fishing enterprises worldwide spent $124 billion to bring in a catch valued at $70 billion. Where did the other $54 billion come from? From governments—from taxpayers—as a subsidy to a dying industry. It would make far more sense to pay that $54 billion to fishermen to stay home and give the world's fish an opportunity to replenish their populations, but that solution is not on the political radar screen. As usual, livestock play a significant role in the destructive dynamic: one-third of the world's catch of fish is turned into fish meal and fed to livestock.

So, as I say, a more vegetarian world is coming, whether we like it or not—or else we will soon encounter a nightmare landscape that will be a grotesque exaggeration of the unfortunate nutritional disparity we see around the globe today. It will be a world in which the rich few eat steak and swordfish while the poor majority literally perish of hunger. Unhappily, that is the direction in which we are currently moving. Since the 1970s, food production of the basic grains and tubers eaten by the world's poor has been growing at a slower rate than that of feed grains for meat that is in turn consumed mostly by the minority of the planet that is well fed.

In China and other "developing" nations, as a segment of society grows rich and begins eating a Western diet, we find that these nations for the first time experience a rise in the incidence of Western ailments. British author Peter Cox explains:

> *While 70 per cent of the protein in average Western diets comes from animals, only 7 per cent of Chinese protein does. While most Chinese suffer very little from the major killer diseases of the West, those affluent Chinese who consume similar amounts of animal protein to Westerners also have the highest rates of heart disease, cancer, and diabetes.*

In the future, we in the West may well experience the reverse dynamic. Even if we don't choose to get ahead of the curve, population and price pressures will eventually force us reluctantly into the greater health that comes from eating lower on the food chain. As our supply of grain grows more precarious and prices increase, we may resort to actually eating our food instead of feeding it to livestock and then find our health bills going down and our longevity increasing.

People often hear conflicting nutritional advice, shrug their shoulders, and decide they might as well eat what they want, or what they're used to, since the experts can't seem to agree on anything anyway. That reaction, of course, is exactly what the meat and dairy industries are praying for. Just as the tobacco industry survives by keeping millions of people addicted to its murderous product, which it until recently claimed was harmless, so the meat and dairy industries thrive by keeping the general population too confused or misinformed to change their destructive eating habits. But the case for the health benefits of a vegetarian diet is at least as clear, and established in at least as many scientific studies, as the case for not smoking. The human body was simply not designed to accommodate tar and nicotine—nor was it designed to process dead animals or products derived from the lactation of other mammals.

Of course, just as some people willingly accept the risk of lung cancer because they profess to enjoy their cigarettes, others may look, if not gladly, then at least with resignation, upon the prospect of heart disease or stroke because they so love their hamburgers. And I suppose we all have the right to kill ourselves if we want to. If only it were that simple. Because we do not have the right to kill the planet. And, as we will see later, the animal-based diet has proven to be as toxic to the Earth as it is to ourselves.

Now I know what most of you are probably thinking. "If this guy's telling me not to eat meat or chicken or fish or eggs or cheese, what the hell's left to eat?"

Hold on to that thought.

First, if I may, I'd like to tell you my story.

# CHAPTER THREE

# Improving on Nature

My great-grandfather owned and operated a mid-sized organic dairy farm outside of Great Falls, Montana. My grandfather took the farm over from him, and my father took it over from my grandfather. I knew from the time I was knee-high to a grasshopper that someday that farm would belong to me and my brother.

When I was three or four years old, my mother used to wake me up at dawn and bring me to the cow barn, in order, I suppose, to have someone to talk to as she milked the cows. One of my earliest memories is of walking too close to the back end of a cow and getting kicked pretty hard. I bounced off a wall and then the cow kicked me again. I still remember thinking: *When will this stop?*

My mother taught me to work from that early age. She would instruct me to collect ladybugs from plants in the garden, count them, and then put them back in the garden. I guess I learned to count that way. It was useless make-work, of course, but this was the era of Roosevelt, and make-work hadn't yet developed a bad reputation.

From the time I was five, I was doing real chores around the farm. Often I worked under the wing of my brother, Dick, who was a year older and a lot bigger. When he wasn't beating me up, he was telling me what to do. It was my job to feed the calves buttermilk, and since we didn't have buckets with nipples in those days, I used my hands. Every weekend I'd have to clean the calf barn of manure; in the winter it froze and that could make the work particularly unpleasant. I still remember a time when I was about seven, working in the fields late on a frigid afternoon. I allowed myself to cry a few tears, and my father told me, "You might as well grit your teeth, because cryin's only going to slow you down, and we're not quittin' till we're finished." It was a lesson I burned into my heart.

At eight or nine I began milking cows and branding calves. At ten I learned how to castrate calves. At harvesttime, I'd work long past dark cutting the grain. I'd rake hay and stack it, and I learned to drive a tractor and a team of horses. I worked every day of the year but two: July Fourth and Christmas. On those days all I had to do was feed the animals—and that took just a few hours, so I looked forward to those holidays with great patriotism and Christian feeling, respectively.

All the years of my childhood, the Lyman family spent cherished evenings together, sitting around and listening to my father read the *Saturday Evening Post* aloud to us. When I was in high school, the family got its first TV. Now we had a new kind of family evening at home: all of us gathered around in the den, watching the test pattern. The future looked bright indeed.

When we weren't farming or getting absorbed in test patterns, Dick and I liked to grab a couple of twenty-two caliber rifles and go out and shoot anything that moved, and a few things that didn't. We shot deer and elk, which we skinned and ate. We shot all kinds of birds: sparrows, crows, magpies, killdeer, curlews, partridge. When we had an infestation of gophers, we shot a thousand in a day. Once, in a particularly renegade mood, we shot the glass insulation off all the local power lines. From our point of view, those damn things were just hanging up there, practically asking for it. It was a point of view the sheriff didn't quite share.

At the end of his sophomore year in high school, Dick developed a swelling of his lymph glands. He was diagnosed with Hodgkin's disease. In those days, the disease was always fatal. We didn't talk about it much in my family, but it was a quiet fact around which much of our lives revolved. From that point on, Dick always did exactly what he wanted to do, and nobody questioned him. He loved the woods more than anything, and he'd go hunting and fishing at the drop of a hat. I stayed behind and did more than my share of the farmwork. When he was a junior in high school, Dick got married, and he had a child in his senior year. He was living hard and fast.

My confidence in my farming future stood behind the disastrous academic record I achieved in high school. I excelled in football, but I didn't do much else well. I cut classes right and left and graduated only, I suspect, because my teachers didn't particularly want to see my mug around anymore. I had always gone to school in the morning with manure on my boots, and my respect for the institution was such that I felt that there was more on my boots on the way home.

So I was delighted to be out of school and back on the farm I loved. But when my father, nervous about the prospect of my someday taking over the 540-acre spread, prevailed upon me to look seriously at all the business aspects of not just working on a farm but actually *running* it, I realized how ill-equipped I was. I lacked most of the skills that were necessary for steering a modern business. I decided to do what any self-respecting red-blooded American boy does who's partied and daydreamed his way through twelve years of school without learning a damn thing: I went to college.

My grandfather had told me that he had connections back East—he claimed he could even get me into Harvard. I had too much respect for the Ivy League to take him up on it. I resolved to handle my future myself. I packed up what I owned, which was about all I had ever owned: one pair of boots, one pair of pants, and two shirts. And I headed off for Montana State University.

I never sent home for money. I covered the cost of all four years of my higher education by playing poker. Although I was pretty good at it, living off poker can be a nip-and-tuck affair. Luckily, I wasn't born with an overly expressive face.

I wasn't about to repeat at university the mistake I had made in high school. This time, I paid attention and did my homework. I took courses at the College of Agriculture. It was an exciting time to be launching into agricultural studies. We learned to spurn the old-fashioned, inefficient methods of farming—the organic methods of my father, grandfather, and great-grandfather. There was not one course offered in organic agriculture. In its place, a bold new age of chemically enhanced agriculture was dawning. We learned the most up-to-date methods of using pesticides and herbicides, hormones and antibiotics. My professors were all chemists and academicians, without an hour's worth of real farming experience among them. These guys were so good at what they did, I figured, they didn't even have to get their hands dirty. I bought it all, hook, line, and sinker.

After college, I signed up for a stint in the Army. Since I had already completed ROTC in college, the Army had no choice but to make me an officer. I found myself having a damn good time. I had to work only five and a half days a week, and I made more money playing poker on my off-time than I got paid for being a soldier. After the kind of work I was used to on the farm, my basic training in Fort Knox was a piece of cake. And I didn't have to worry about the weather, or the price of milk. When I was hungry, they fed me. The accommodations were fine, especially at the Hunter-Leget base in California, where it never got cold, and the bullshit never froze. As much as I loved farming, I had to admit, the Army had it beat for sheer pleasure. If my brother hadn't been sick, I probably would have made a career of it.

But my brother was dying, and I came home. Dick could hardly work; my father was getting older and was burdened with more than he could handle. He didn't cope with stress very well. He needed me to run the farm. I studied the farm's books, which now I could decipher, and I suddenly understood something that had simply never occurred to me before. We were poor. My old man was barely making ends meet. I told him that if I was going to take over this operation, I sure as hell wasn't going to keep running it on a hand-to-mouth basis as an organic dairy farm. I was going to deficit-finance, expand, and employ all the brand-new chemical farming techniques I'd learned about in college.

My father had no choice. He handed over the farm. But as he shook my hand on the deal, he had a few short words for me.

He told me I was wrong.

Crop rotation was the first principle of the old-fashioned organic method of dairy farming employed by my father, grandfather, and great-grandfather. A field that was used to grow alfalfa one year got planted with, say, wheat the next, and corn the following year. Farmers paid particular attention to nitrogen-fixing crops, like beans or clover or alfalfa, which pulled nitrogen out of the air and put it into the soil, thus naturally fertilizing it. The second principle was leaving fields fallow, usually at least once every few years. Doing so restored moisture in the soil, made weeding simple, and let the microorganisms and earthworms in the soil go to work regenerating it. The third principle, analogous to the second but concerning animal husbandry, was best expressed in the old farmer's saying: "When you raise an animal on grass, take half and leave half." In other words, don't let your cattle overgraze. By leaving roughly half the grass alive in the grazing field, the grass would come back each year and its roots would hold the soil and protect it from erosion.

Finally, farming organically meant working with Nature, not against it. Organic agriculture is predicated on doing things on Nature's time frame. Crops are harvested when they're ripe, and fields are cut into small sections so that each crop can be picked at its peak condition.

These were quaint old ways, and I guess I thought they were good enough for people who didn't know any better, but they sure as hell weren't good enough for an educated young farmer like me. Those of us who had been schooled in the ways of the Green Revolution were going to bury these old methods of farming the way electricity had buried the kerosene lamp. There was a better living to be had through chemistry.

I found beauty in the almost mathematical precision of the new chemical agriculture. I would take a hollow tube, three feet long and maybe an inch in diameter, and press it into the ground to obtain a soil sample. By bringing this sample to a soil-testing lab, I could determine which of the three basic soil nutrients—nitrogen, phosphorus, and potassium—were needed in the soil, at what depths and in what percentages. Since our soil was already potassium-rich, I might be advised to buy some eighty-pound bags of "11-48-0," a fertilizer mixture that was 11 percent nitrogen, 48 percent phosphorus, and 0 percent potassium. Later I began buying fertilizer in bulk, two or three hundred tons at a time. I'd spread the fields with this mixture and it would seep down into the soil like a timed-release medicine.

Fertilizing this way worked like a dream, especially after I'd had a few years to fiddle around and discover the best mixtures. I found that by loading the soil with about a hundred pounds per acre of "33-0-0" in the spring, and then "rotating" that with an equivalent amount of "16-20-0" in the fall, I was doubling the yields per acre of all our crops. And I didn't have to waste any acreage by leaving it fallow.

I handled the problem of weeds with something called 2-4 D, a chemical weed-control product. I just sprayed it throughout the farm, covering five or six hundred acres a day. If a little was good, more was better. Before long I was looking for new and more powerful concoctions of 2-4 D. Then I began using an excellent variety of herbicide called 2-4-5 T. In Vietnam they called it Agent Orange.

Once I had the extra crop yield, of course, I was faced with the problem of what to do with it. With the occasional exception of wheat, none of the crops I was raising fetched much of a price on the market. They were more useful as livestock feed, but it was more feed than I needed for the fifty head of cattle I then had. You didn't have to be a brain surgeon to come up with the solution: buy more cattle.

After I acquired more cattle than I could possibly allow to graze on my fields, I simply put them in confinement and converted a grazing operation into a feedlot. I corralled the animals in roofless pens, a hundred or two hundred in each, with a trough for feed on one side of the pen. And I embraced the fundamental challenge of the feedlot operator: make the cattle grow as big and fat as possible, as quickly as possible. You get paid by the pound, after all. Cattle don't win any prizes by keeping their figures. The more grain you feed them, the fattier and therefore the more tender and pricey their meat becomes, so I learned how to alter my cattle's natural dietary habits. Whereas my father and grandfather raised cattle almost completely on grass and roughage, I now cut out their grazing rights and fed them only roughage, grain, and protein concentrates, gradually increasing the percentage of grain until they were 90 percent grain-fed. This made their meat extremely fatty and gave it the nice white flecks you see in the better cuts of beef in your grocery stores.

This diet also, unfortunately, upsets the cow's natural digestive system, which was designed for grass, not grain. As a consequence of the digestive stress, many of my animals suffered vaginal and rectal prolapses—organs that belonged on the inside of the cow fell out of them. It was too expensive to call a vet every time this happened, so I spent countless hours stuffing twenty-five pounds of cow back inside the animal and then sewing the wound, the whole force of a six-hundred-pound heifer straining against me.

I have been out of cattle farming for fifteen years now, and I will go back to it the day I wake up with a burning desire to perform another bovine rectal prolapse operation.

While I was expanding my feedlot operation, I would acquire cattle at auction. I might get a hundred head at a single auction, from maybe twenty different sources. After transporting them to my ranch, I put them one at a time into a chute to restrain them. Then I cut off their horns, branded them, vaccinated them for various diseases, castrated the males, and locked them in a pen. Unfortunately, with so many animals from different origins concentrated close together, disease became my worst enemy. When I shifted from a grazing operation to a feedlot, the health problems of my herd rose dramatically.

It was a constant battle: Economics versus Nature. If you don't catch a cow during the first few days it's symptomatic, there's about a 50 percent chance it'll die on you. If even 5 percent of your cattle die, there's no way you'll ever make a profit. Unfortunately, cattle in confinement develop more diseases than you can possibly vaccinate against. In an enclosed space like a cattle pen, even those afflicted cows that successfully respond to a vaccination can pass the germ to other cattle in the process of shedding the disease. So, like most feedlot operators, I learned to put antibiotics in the cattle's feed. It would have been too time-consuming to try to target only the sick cattle with the antibiotic-enhanced feed, and anyway I never knew which cow might get sick tomorrow. It was much easier and more logical to simply put the antibiotics in the feed of all the cattle. Here again, like all other feedlot operators, I was outsmarted by Nature, which endowed the bacteria causing these diseases with the capacity to mutate and gain immunity to any antibiotic science can develop. If you use antibiotics sparingly, this is a manageable problem. But once you begin to use them liberally, adding increasing amounts to animal feed and then injecting more into those cattle that nonetheless fall sick, you invite the resistance that will defeat you over time. Soon I found myself changing antibiotics in the feed every thirty days or so, and they were becoming less and less effective. Constantly experimenting with new and larger quantities of antibiotics at an escalating cost, I felt that I was on a treadmill and had to keep running faster just to stay in place.

Sometimes the drugs that I used to inoculate cattle were eventually determined to be dangerous to human health and were banned. But the government always seemed to be sufficiently cooperative with agribusiness to make sure that the stockpiles of the suspect drug inventoried by the drug companies were sold before the ban went into effect. Once the banned drugs were in farmers' hands, they were used until exhausted.

After bovine diseases in their various forms, flies constitute the greatest hazard to feedlot operations. With every cow in a pen producing twenty-five pounds of manure in a day, the flies can get so thick that they actually threaten a cow's ability to breathe. And cows, restlessly trying to do something about the flies persecuting them, sometimes kick up so much dust that they can contract what is called dust pneumonia. But the great promise of chemical agriculture is that every problem represents merely another challenge to science. And the scientific fix for the fly problem was insecticide. Early in the morning I would fill up a fly fogger with insecticide and spray great clouds of it over the whole operation. The insecticide would of course fall into the feed and the water of the cattle, as well as on the trees and the grass and the crops. In addition, I treated the animals for grubs–the wormlike larvae of certain insects–by covering their backs with insecticides that were absorbed through the skin in order to kill the fly eggs. Naturally, I had neither the time nor the inclination to think about the possibility of this deadly chemical passing through the hide into the tissues that would become somebody's dinner.

I handled the chemical operations on the farm without any gloves, goggles, or protective clothing. We young farmers had been taught a lot of marvelous new things at Montana State University, but we hadn't been taught that the products we were using were a danger to our health.

To make the cattle grow faster, I didn't restrict myself to merely forcing upon them an unnatural diet of grain. Like most cattle farmers today, I used hormones to stimulate the growth of the animals. These growth hormones are similar to the steroids that misguided muscle-builders use at significant risk to their own health. The hormones were either added to the feed, injected directly into the animals, or implanted underneath their hides in the form of timed-release pellets. For years, the hormone I used most frequently was diethylstilbestrol, or DES. I used it not only to stimulate growth but also to abort pregnant heifers. (After all, the added weight of a fetus would have been wasted, since it wasn't going to become hamburger.) During the years that I used the hormone, the debate raged over whether or not DES could be carcinogenic to humans. Finally, in 1977, the government banned the use of DES, but since it was so cheap and effective, many feedlot operators bought up as much product as possible for use after it was no longer available for sale. I regret to say that I was one of them. After my DES ran out, about two years after the ban went into effect, I continued to use a whole bunch of new and improved growth hormones. In those days, I never met a chemical I didn't like.

It was also illegal to use growth hormones on any cattle that would be slaughtered within two weeks of ingesting or being treated with them. This was not exactly a law that I obeyed religiously, and I don't think many other feedlot operators did. In fact, at the current time, all European Union countries ban the import of American beef because of our continued use of growth hormones.

Most Americans don't have any idea of the extraordinary lengths the Department of Agriculture goes to in its mission to protect the grower at the expense of the consumer. When a chemical is banned from use, a farmer or livestock operator who has the chemical in stock has a choice: either to lose money by disposing of the product, or to use it and take the risk of getting caught breaking the law. How severe is that risk? Well, if you use a banned product in your cattle feed, you have to face the prospect that the government is going to inspect one out of every two hundred fifty thousand carcasses. They will test this carcass not for all banned substances, but just for a small fraction of them. And even if they detect some residue of a banned substance, and even if they're able to trace the carcass to the ranch that produced it, the guilty rancher is likely at most to receive a stern letter with a strongly worded warning. I never met a rancher who suffered in any way from breaking any regulation meant to protect the safety of our meat. The whole procedure is, in short, a charade.

I didn't lose too much sleep over breaking the rules.

I had bigger worries.

More and more, I had to worry about money. Even though I had increased crop yields dramatically, even though I could now grow a heifer to eleven hundred pounds in just fifteen months instead of the thirty months it used to take, even though I had bought out or leased many of my neighbors' farms and increased my acreage fortyfold, it was getting harder and harder to make ends meet. The chemicals themselves were expensive, and every year I had to use more chemical fertilizer and more antibiotics to get the same result as the year before. And the cattle continued to get sick and sometimes die in spite of my best efforts.

I was working eighteen-hour days, and feeling less and less secure financially. My only stress-relieving social entertainment consisted of poker games once or twice a month in the winter. I played with a group of about ten men, almost all farmers, and all serious beer drinkers. The games were pure relaxation for all of us, at low stakes. Most of us had already placed a high-stakes bet on chemical agriculture, and we didn't have the stomach for much more betting.

I had dug myself into a chemical pit so deep I didn't have time to do anything except keep digging. When my brother died of cancer in 1969, I lost a valuable sounding board. I had taken full control of the Lyman Ranch shortly thereafter, buying out my parents' stake, and ever since there had been no check on my actions. Only my wife, Willow Jeane, whom I had married in the early years of the transformation of the farm, would occasionally comment to me: "Are you sure we're going in the right direction?" She would note that the trees were starting to die, and that in spite of the herbicides, the weed problem seemed to be getting worse. And she wasn't at all pleased the day I came in with so much herbicide on my clothing that my mere presence killed off the houseplants.

I used to have a regular business lunch once a week in Great Falls with a group of about fifteen Montana feedlot operators. We were all devotees of the new school of chemical agriculture and we figured that by getting together and sharing our experiences we could help each other find the right technological solution for every problem we encountered. We didn't question the underlying theology of our revolution: there would always be a magic chemical bullet to cure whatever problems we ran into. We stuck by that theology in spite of the mounting evidence that every bullet just seemed to cause more problems.

Of those fifteen feedlot operators who were in business fifteen years ago, I believe that just one may still be in business today. Our challenge had been to defeat Nature. And we found that we could do it.

But only by destroying the land, and with it, ourselves.

# Chapter Four

# From the Farm to the Capital

There's never been a moment in the thirty-three years of my marriage that I've regretted getting wed. My wife can't say the same, but then, I married better than she did. Early on, Willow Jeane and I devised a system of shared responsibility: I make the big decisions and she makes the little decisions. One of the little decisions she gets to make is deciding which are the big decisions and which are the little decisions. An example of a big decision she often assigned to me over the years was what to have for dinner. Now, I've got to admit, I didn't used to appreciate just how profound a decision that was. I've learned the hard way.

Willow Jeane was a widow with three children when I met her, and I was a content, gainfully employed, fourth-generation Montana farmer. And I knew right off I needed her more than she needed me. But until I met her, I had no idea I needed anyone.

Willow Jeane doesn't panic easily. One time, around 1968, she was on a flight from Phoenix to Great Falls. She was flying alone, knitting me a sweater. She looked out the window and saw flames coming from an engine. Before long, three of the plane's four engines were on fire. Willow Jeane just kept knitting. The woman sitting next to her shouted: "How can you just keep knitting with the plane on fire?" Willow Jeane said, "Well, I figure there isn't much I can do about it, and I have to get this sweater finished."

I've seen terror in her eyes only once. It was a winter's night in 1979, eleven years into our marriage. We'd added two more children by then to the three we already had, and the farm had grown into an agribusiness of ten thousand acres and seven thousand head of cattle and up to thirty employees. I was lying in a hospital bed, facing an emergency operation for a tumor that had been found that same day in my spine. Willow Jeane's first husband had died of cancer when he was twenty-eight, and the prospect of widowhood once more was a bit much even for her. For my part, I was damned sure I was going to survive, but my surgeon, known around the hospital as Old Cut-and-Run, had told me not to expect to walk again.

I'd had a bad back for twenty years, but I never liked doctors much, so I'd simply decided to live with it. I could never sleep more than two hours at a time before the pain would wake me, so I'd just get up and walk around with a book in my hands for a couple more hours till my back could take the strain of bed again. Some folks might go to a doctor for a condition like that, but the thought didn't cross my mind. I got a lot of reading done. Besides, I was smoking three packs a day, and that's a hard pace to keep up if you waste too much time sleeping.

My condition was more or less stable until I went on vacation with my family—the second vacation we ever took—to the Black Hills of South Dakota. We stayed in a hotel with a pool–that was a real treat for us–and near the pool we came across something I'd never seen before: a hot tub. After I'd been soaking in it about a minute, I felt a sensation in my back like a grenade exploding. In retrospect, that hot tub may have saved my life, but I haven't stepped into one since, and don't plan on doing so.

By the time I got back to the ranch, still in exquisite pain, I'd developed another symptom: I couldn't feel my feet hit the ground when I walked. For a moment I thought this might have meant that I'd become a very important person. But then I looked down and saw that I was in fact still walking upon the ground; I just couldn't *feel* it. I kept putting my feet down wrong and spraining my ankles. After this happened enough times, I knew I had to bite the bullet and see a doctor.

The doctor hit my knee with a hammer and then looked at me.

"How do you do that?" he asked, astonished.

"Do what?" I said.

"You have no reflex."

"Well, I've never been the jumpy sort."

"I'm afraid you've either got a tumor or MS."

This was exactly why I didn't go to doctors.

He sent me to a neurologist, who ran me through some simple dexterity tests and ruled out multiple sclerosis. That pretty much ruled in a tumor. I was rushed to a hospital. The snow was coming down hard. The nurses ran a myelogram on me–sent some fluid down my spine. On a monitor, you could see the fluid travel down the spinal cord and then stop when it reached the tumor, which was about the size of my thumb, and I've got big thumbs. The attending physician recommended that I be rushed into surgery; a certain Dr. X. was on hand to perform it. Now I'd known Dr. X. a long time, and I'd known his reputation. I wouldn't let the man castrate a goat. I said, forget it, and I got on the phone and called my old friend Alex.

Alex was a tall, skinny, rawboned man of about sixty. A cattle rancher from Fort Benton, about fifty miles north of Great Falls, he was also the finest surgeon in Montana. He loved ranching, loved roping, loved the land. Nothing about him looked or sounded like a doctor—until he took off the gloves he always wore on his ranch. His hands gave him away. One look at his hands, and if you didn't guess surgeon, you'd guess concert pianist. I've never held a man in higher regard. I'd known him long enough to know he never bothered a soul in his life. If you didn't need him, he wasn't around. If you needed him, he was on you like stink. He was that kind of guy.

The storm had escalated into a blizzard and Alex said there was no way he could make it to the hospital that night, but he'd be down at dawn if he had to call in a helicopter. He assured me that I did, in fact, have a major problem. If the tumor was inside the cord, there was less than one chance in a million I'd walk again. But as long as I could move my feet, the operation could wait till morning. If I found I couldn't move my feet, I'd better let Dr. X. go ahead and operate.

I stayed up all night, moving my feet and thinking. I was thinking about what counted and what didn't.

Having ten thousand acres didn't count.

Having seven thousand head of cattle didn't count.

Having thirty trucks and twenty tractors and seven combines didn't count.

Having a $5-million-a-year agribusiness didn't count.

The pleasure of writing million-dollar checks didn't count. My family counted, and the land counted.

For some reason, I kept thinking about the soil—the magnetic feel of cool, dark, loamy, worm-laden soil in my hands. I'd grown up with my hands in that soil, and I'd always liked the feeling so much, I rarely troubled to wash them. As a boy, I once went over to the house of a friend whose mother was a stickler for hygiene, and when she gave me the choice of washing the dirt off my hands or not eating supper, it was a no-brainer. I just didn't eat.

Suspecting that I would never walk again, yet finding it hard to truly accept this probability, I found myself wondering what kind of invalid I would make. Would I just go around feeling sorry for myself, or would I be able to move forward with my life? Would I be able to run a ten-thousand-acre farm from within the confines of a wheelchair? It didn't seem likely.

Willow Jeane is the most adaptable person I've ever met in my life. She was a town girl who had learned to milk, feed, and brand cows. She was a complete partner; we'd worked together on the ranch full time during the day, and built our house together at night. She was cool and calm and collected even that day, revealing her terror only in her eyes. I could depend on her for virtually anything—but to raise a family of five and run an agribusiness this size with little help from an invalid husband . . . I couldn't ask that.

This was the first night I hadn't slept beside her since we were married.

I kept moving my feet, and my thoughts kept returning to how rich the soil had looked when I was a kid. It didn't look like that anymore. Now it crumbled in my hands. It was as thin as sand. There were no more worms in it. After all the tons of herbicides and pesticides and chemical fertilizer I'd poured into it, the soil looked more like asbestos. The trees on and around the farm were dying. The birds were gone. The farm was no longer a living, breathing thing; it was an increasingly precarious chemical equation. I made up my mind then and there that no matter what the outcome of my operation, I'd dedicate the rest of my life to restoring the land to what it had been when I'd had the good fortune to be born to it.

I didn't close my eyes for a moment that night. I thought about how I would know, upon waking after the operation, if it had been successful. The nurses would surely tell me it had gone well, and probably offer some vague bromides of encouragement. But I had a need to learn immediately the truth about whether I would walk again, as if it would re- quire every last moment of my life's energy to defeat the de- pression that would surely set in if the likely happened. How could I figure out the truth, I wondered, watching my feet swing back and forth—and there I had my answer. My feet would let me know.

At the stroke of dawn, I heard a nurse say, "Here comes Old Cut-and-Run," and, good as clockwork, Alex strode into the room. He was never known for wasting a word. He didn't say much to me beyond cussing at me for spoiling his weekend. And I was wheeled into surgery.

I awoke the next day in the intensive care unit, propped up on my side. The first thing I did was to look down at my feet. I threw off the sheet to expose them; then, with some effort, I was able to slide down the bed so that they could reach the metal bars at its foot. I felt the metal. It was cold to the touch. It was the most euphoric sensation I've ever known in my life. A nurse hurried over and tried to move me back up in the bed. I told her there was no way in the world she could get me to move.

Alex was in the room by the break of day. He explained that, after cutting the bone off the outside of my spinal column, he had discovered that the tumor was not only inside the cord but also extended beneath it. His only option was to pick a nerve, cut the nerve, and hope the tumor was attached to it like a fish on a line. Alex picked one, cut it, and I escaped paralysis with a one-in-a-million operation. He didn't seem as surprised or moved as I was by that fact. My miracle was simply his day's work. All the same, he was as attentive and concerned as a doctor could possibly be. For two days, he made sure I had no residual feeling loss, checked to see that I was getting excellent care from the nursing staff, satisfied himself that I was in good spirits. Then, certain that the operation was an unqualified success and that there was nothing further he could do for me, he up and disappeared, without so much as a parting word. Old Cut-and-Run had lived up to his name.

Once I knew I would walk again, I remembered the promise that I had made to myself the night before the operation. I confess I may have winced a bit upon remembering it. Restoring my land to a healthy state was a hell of a project, after all the punishment I'd put it through. Still, I had, after all, made that damned vow. I thought about saying *just kidding,* but even I had enough integrity not to let myself off the hook that easily. I knew I had a sacred obligation to undo the harm I had done to the land. I just didn't have a clue how to go about it.

After a week's stay in the hospital, my friend Joe gave me a ride home. I'll never forget that ride, and I doubt I'll ever understand it. As we drove along, I felt as if the world had accelerated wildly, and that we were cruising at something approaching warp speed. I kept yelling at Joe to slow down. He tried to comply, but eventually he could only laugh at me. We were apparently doing fifteen miles an hour, and there I was, still terrified at the velocity.

I don't know what that fear was about—whether I was ill or whether my brain was trying to send me some sort of message—but I do know that life slowed down for me considerably during my convalescence at home. Walking was of course arduous at first, and the pain resulting from going up and down any kind of steps was excruciating. But it was my eyes that presented me with my worst problem. They had suddenly lost focus; I was seeing double. It was troubling to see two of everything, and downright scary whenever my mother-in-law visited. I called Alex and asked him what could be causing the problem. His reaction was memorable: "Beats the hell out of me. Wasn't nothin' I did. I operated on your *back*, remember?" Eventually, another doctor reassured me that the problem was probably caused by a virus, and gave me that magical blessing that seems to be the most important lesson of any medical education: "It'll go away."

There was a strange symbolism to my recent plight that I would have paid good money not to consider. Life was speeding by, and I had lost focus. Unfortunately, there was nothing to do *but* consider what it might have meant. After all, with my eyes out of focus, I couldn't read, couldn't watch TV, couldn't work. And so I sat and thought, and took a long-postponed inventory of myself.

I didn't much like what I found in the mirror: a couple of cold-blooded twins with a blurry but distinct resemblance to me. I saw, in lamentable duplicate, a relentlessly calculating individual who did whatever was necessary to achieve his end. Instead of making decisions with Willow Jeane, I'd been making them myself, then discussing them with her simply in order to get her to buy into my view of things. I'd fired employees at the drop of a hat. If a worker didn't get the job done fast enough, or showed up late, or failed to observe some specified maintenance procedure with the farm equipment, he was history; I wouldn't think twice about giving him the ax. I had never taken the time to train my employees, never tried to understand their side of any issue. And if I had little compassion for my workers, I had none at all for the animals I prepared for slaughter. They existed for my profit, and my profit alone. I was a no-good SOB, and I couldn't imagine why anyone would think otherwise. I was amazed that a person as good as my wife had married me. I wondered whether she might have simply taken me on as a project.

There was an expression—some might say a platitude—I had often voiced in the past: "If you're not high on yourself, who else can be?" Well, after taking a good look in the mirror, I wasn't very high on myself. And so I had a choice: I could either spend the rest of my life as a selfish, sour person, or I could rectify what I didn't like about myself. I decided to adopt the philosophy—nonsensical as it might sound—that I had a second chance to make a first impression.

My priorities changed before my unsteady eyes. Life and health came first; business and profits lost considerable status. Compassion at last entered the equation as I began to suspect that my disregard for animals as living creatures was somehow related to my disregard for my fellow human beings.

I remembered a time when my wife and I were sorting out fattened, top-end Charolais cattle for market. I was about to load a 1,400-pound white steer onto the truck when Willow Jeane stopped me. She said, "This one's so beautiful, let's let it go in the next load." I deferred to her reluctantly. In the morning, we found that steer dead. Had it made it onto the truck alive, it would have been worth about seven hundred fifty dollars, and it would have been someone else's problem had it died en route to slaughter. Instead, it was worthless. I had the animal skinned, its hide tanned, and put the tanned hide on the back of our couch. Every time I had looked at that hide before my illness, I could think only about the senseless loss of seven hundred fifty dollars. Now I looked at that same hide and felt, oddly enough, some trace of pity for an animal that I used to regard as an economic unit.

It's easy to talk about making a transition from an economic view of animal life to a compassionate view of animals as individual, living creatures, but it's a hard thing to do when your ability to support your family depends upon efficiently turning those creatures into carcasses. And so I refrained, at the time, from exploring the possible ramifications of my newfound sympathy toward animals, or from asking myself the big questions about whether raising cattle for slaughter was ultimately a defensible calling. Instead I focused my mind's eye on the challenge, monumental enough, of pursuing that calling with a renewed respect for the land.

In common with most ranchers who grew crops for their herds, weeds caused me far more problems than insects or weather or anything else, and at that time I must have been spraying a hundred times more herbicide than insecticide.

The worst offender was a devil of a weed called leafy spurge. It emits a natural toxin which kills surrounding crops that compete with it for water and nutrients. If I was truly going to revamp my farming methods to protect the land, my priority had to be attacking the weed problem in a new way.

I was not alone in my losing battle against weeds. When I announced the formation of a local weed-control group to look at alternatives to the chemical war on weeds, the response was tremendous. A hundred fifty farmers showed up in the middle of a blizzard to take part in a discussion of new approaches to weed management. We talked about methods of biological and mechanical weed control, and integrated pest management. Since a weed is nothing more than a plant out of place, we discussed the possibility of tracing a plant to its origins and researching the natural control agents that keep the plant from proliferating in its native environment. We didn't know all the answers, but at least we each knew we weren't alone in our frustration with chemical techniques.

Meanwhile, I talked with a bank officer about getting a loan that would enable me to make the transition to the kind of farming that would restore the land. I would need capital to rebuild the soil with compost, rock dust, and "green manure"–a crop such as clover grown and plowed back down in order to fix nitrogen from the air and put it into the soil. The banker asked me why I wanted to do this. I told him that I was attempting to practice something very old: farming in association with Nature.

"What the hell does that mean?" he asked.

"I want to become an organic farmer," I said.

He looked at me with astonishment.

"And you want my help?"

"Yes."

"It won't happen, Lyman," he said. "Turning the clock back to this organic business will never work, and I've got other customers who wouldn't care for it." He meant the chemical dealer, the pharmaceutical dealer, the fertilizer dealer—all of whom I was effectively cutting out of the action. "We have a system here that functions just fine and you're asking to mess with it."

I started then to glimpse the interconnectedness of banking, factory farming, and the giant chemical and pharmaceutical firms. We farmers were caught in a kind of corporate straitjacket. I felt like I had just gotten myself thrown out of a big fraternity, and for the first time it occurred to me that ultimately I had to get out of farming. I knew I had a big fight on my hands, and my farm with its spiraling debts wasn't the most strategic ground from which to wage it.

It was around this time that my eyes regained their focus. I put them to some of the best work they have ever done: I read Rachel Carson's *Silent Spring*. Published in 1962, it remains a timeless wake-up call to the nation. From the point of view of the chemical industry, the book must be like one of those annoying car alarms that just won't shut off. It should be required reading for every high school student in America, not to mention every farmer. I wish I had read the book before I began my career in farming, instead of picking it up only after I had decided to get out. When Carson wrote so movingly of the dangers of pesticides to our rivers and to wildlife and to human health, 637,666,000 pounds of the synthetic poisons were being produced a year. Today, as Vice President Gore points out, production of these toxins has increased by 400 percent, and the harm they do is cumulative. In Carson's words: "This pollution is for the most part irrecoverable; the chain of evil it initiates not only in the world that must support life but in living tissues is for the most part irreversible."

Along with the other members of my weed-control group, I began to lobby the state legislature to fund a new, small facility at Montana State University to conduct research into biological pest and weed control. You would think that this would be a harmless political cause, but the chemical industry fought us every step of the way. They played hardball, threatening the funding of various departments throughout the university system if this little research facility was created. The university consequently became wary of getting too closely involved with those of us who were pushing biological approaches to agricultural problems. The chemical industry certainly acted as if it was scared of something. Luckily, the chairman of the relevant legislative committee was from Corvallis, the town where the satellite facility would be built, and he was happy to bring home the pork.

Eventually our weed-control group hired a graduate student in agriculture to help develop a biologically sound way to control leafy spurge. We found that Romania was the weed's country of origin, and since leafy spurge was not a problem there, we deduced that a natural control agent must exist. We sent our student to Romania, and he came back triumphantly with a collection of beetles and other insects that would eventually help us combat the problem. On my own farm I implemented integrated pest management practices and, at the sign of a pest like weevils, chose to harvest my crops early rather than spray.

I had never had a political bone in my body. I wouldn't

have been able to tell you at the time if I was a Democrat or a Republican, and I'm not sure that I ever bothered reading a flyer, much less delivering one. But my involvement in the seemingly nonpartisan cause of battling weeds nontoxically was giving me, willy-nilly, a political education. When the Montana Agricultural Extension Service (a program of the Department of Agriculture) asked me to co-chair its effort to increase its state funding, I agreed to lobby the legislature for the group with the condition that its priorities be reorganized. They agreed, and the results of our efforts were not only an increase in the funding of the state's Extension Service but an allocation of millions of dollars into research on biological weed control. Today Montana may well lead the nation in biological weed control.

I got another political lesson when a friend called and asked me to take a look at the Deaf and Blind School in Great Falls. I had passed it many times but had never poked my head inside. When I did so at my friend's request, I saw that it was in abysmal condition—the whole building rotting, the children passing their days in unsafe and unsanitary conditions. I told my friend that I would do what I could to help get a new school built, thinking I had a chit to call in with the governor, whom I knew well. But he offered only sympathy, claiming that his fiscal hands were tied. I learned then that relationships weren't nearly as important in the world of politics as leverage. I decided to take my request to the state senator who was chairman of the Long-Range Building Committee, which controlled funds that the governor relied upon for his own pet projects. With the state senator's support, I got $7 million allocated for a new Deaf and Blind School, and I'm proud to say it stands today in Great Falls, Montana, a monument to pure political leverage.

One day, I was griping to Willow Jeane about politicians, and she uttered a sentence she came to regret mightily: "If you're not going to do something about it, then you have no right to complain." So I ran for Congress. Since it turned out that I was a registered Democrat, I entered the 1982 Democratic primary for Montana's eastern congressional district (now Montana has only one district), and to my surprise, I won. As I told my equally astonished wife on our victorious primary night, if I won the general election as well, we'd finally be off the farm, as Willow Jeane dearly wanted. On the other hand, the prospect of being a congressman's wife, with all its attendant limelight, was not exactly her idea of fun. Anticipating a move to Washington, I began to wind down the feedlot, drastically reducing my number of head of cattle. I needed to minimize the managerial requirements of running a farm at the same time I was running a campaign.

My general election campaign was based on three basic themes: Clean Air, Clean Water, and Clean Food. We developed a coalition based not on political ideology but on concern for the land we farmed, the air we breathed, and the water we drank. Montana's voters may not have been ready to support a campaign centered on organic farming, but they did—and do—have an abiding concern for the environment, and they understood intuitively when I made the point that family farming could restore the land that factory farming was destroying. I caught people's attention as a candidate who was a factory farmer taking the side of the family farmers. I wasn't pointing a finger at someone else; I was pointing at myself—I had met the enemy and it was me. I believed then and I believe now that family farms ought to be considered our greatest natural resource and that the fundamental healthfulness of our food and the long-term health of our economy are closely tied to their well-being. I called for programs targeted to help family farms and all farms that withdrew from polluting practices. With the momentum gained by having won an upset victory in the Democratic primary, my campaign caught fire, and I like to think it scared the hell out of the petrochemical industry. Republican and Independent voters were coming my way as often as Democrats. The campaign had nothing to do with party affiliation; it had everything to do with the basic value of respect for the land. And then, as the polls showed me pulling ahead with six weeks to go in the race, my bank suddenly foreclosed on my farm. This development caught me by surprise, although I suspect my opponent may have been more prepared for it. Typically, my bank would simply roll over the debt of any farmer like myself who had more than ample value in the land as collateral, but for some reason in the heat of the campaign the bank saw fit to foreclose. The headlines made people wonder: if this guy can't run his own farm, should we send him to Washington to represent us? I dropped precipitously in the polls when that story came out, then started coming back, but I didn't have enough time to regain all the ground and wound up losing 52 percent to 48 percent.

A year later, in order to settle all my debts, I sold the farm to a Hutterite colony, leaving myself with only my great-grandfather's homestead, which had been its nucleus. In 1987, I was invited to work as a lobbyist for the National Farmers Union in Washington, D.C., and Willow Jeane and I moved to the nation's capital. I didn't get there as a politician, but as someone paid to twist politicians' arms.

Initially I felt like a country bumpkin surrounded by

bright, slick, highly qualified bureaucrats, lawyers, lobbyists, and congressional staffers. I was probably an entertaining spectacle for them. Looking as if I fell off a turnip truck, I was perhaps the sole lobbyist in the District with only one suit. I was also probably the only lobbyist in town who believed in the American civics book view of government—that voters elect representatives to speak for them in office, and that the interests of his or her constituency are an officeholder's paramount concern.

Slowly but surely, though, I learned to play the Beltway game. While much that I gleaned could make a person cynical, there was one heartening lesson at the center of it all: the key to having any degree of success in Washington is, believe it or not, hard work and honesty. Your currency on the Hill is your word; as soon as your word is devalued, you are lost. I made sure not to make any promises I couldn't keep. I never even promised Willow Jeane I'd get a second suit; I just said I was open to considering it. I considered it long and hard, and bought another sport coat.

While working for the National Farmers Union, I naturally lobbied to maintain or increase many farm subsidies. At the time, I believed that this was the best way to help small farmers. I agitated for subsidies that were structured in such a way as to help family farmers more than factory farmers. Certainly, our system of subsidizing farmers seemed complex, bureaucratic, and expensive, but it was the only system we had and my job was to make it work better for my constituency: family farmers.

Another issue I went to work on was the National Organic Production Act of 1990. The purpose of this piece of legislation was to create a uniform, enforceable system of standards by which food could be labeled "organic," so that when a consumer saw that label he or she could know what it meant and trust that it was representing itself honestly. The multinational Con Agra wanted to label beef "organic" if the entity that owned factory-raised cattle for only, say, the last six weeks of its life, didn't further adulterate it with hormones and other chemical products. That wasn't my idea of *organic* and I don't think it was the consumer's idea. Organic foods were then and remain now the fastest-growing segment of the food market, and the bill was designed to regulate this exploding industry and prevent unjustifiable claims from undermining it.

The only problem was that the bill was considered by Capitol Hill insiders to be destined for defeat. Petrochemical interests were lined up against it, and the first rule for most members of Congress is: when in doubt, vote no. I knew that if those of us behind the bill worked diligently to crank up support from our troops—the organic farmers, the health food businesses, maybe some health activists and consumer groups—the end result would simply be a countervailing increase in the lobbying and pressure tactics of the petrochemical industry. So I chose instead to let the bill look as if it was going to die a quick and painless death. Meanwhile, shortly before the vote was scheduled, I went to my friends in organized labor, with whom farm groups had formed a coalition that met regularly on the Hill. Organic standards was not an issue high on the list of Big Labor's concerns, but they had nothing against it. They went to bat for us on the day of the vote. Labor's representatives were at the door of the House chamber giving the members a thumbs-up on the bill. We needed the urban constituency, and now we had it. Members hadn't heard enough from the other side to feel that it was a risky vote.

We caught our opponents asleep at the switch, and the result was the passage of the Organic Production Act of 1990. The White House, which had opposed the measure, went nuts with frustration, since the bill was tied to an appropriations bill that President Bush wanted and needed to sign. And so he reluctantly signed the Organic Production Act into law on November 28, 1990.

It was a heady victory, and I still believe that ultimately it can and will serve some good purpose. But I'd be disingenuous if I didn't also acknowledge that, as of this writing, the national organic standards have yet to be codified by the Department of Agriculture and put into effect. Such are the frustrations of trying to bring about change in Washington, D.C. It's definitely not impossible, and it's always worth trying, but more and more I've come to feel that most fundamental changes in this country come from the grass roots, from the bottom up, and the game Washington plays best is catch-up.

One summer day in Washington in 1990, during the low-key campaign for the Organic Production Act, I was sitting with my feet up on my desk, looking out at the Potomac. The humidity was 98 percent, and it was hot enough to make a mosquito sweat. I started thinking about all the issues, personal and political, that were concerning me. I was feeling a growing sense of cynicism about my work, and about the chances to effect change through legislation. I'd lived through the relentless decline of the family farm. I knew that most of the bureaucratic subsidies I was fighting for went to the raising of feed crops, not human food. I'd read a whole host of depressing statistics about the loss of rain forest throughout the world, and I knew that the lion's share of that rain forest loss came about in order to clear land for cattle grazing. I'd read, too, that livestock outnumber humans on the planet by five to one. I'd learned that about 50 percent of our water usage in this country is dedicated to the production of meat, and that our natural aquifers were being depleted at an alarming rate. I'd learned that we were losing topsoil at a rate of one inch every sixteen years, and that much of that loss of topsoil was related to cattle grazing and to the chemically intensive methods that factory farmers were using (and that I had once used). I'd seen rivers polluted from the waste of cattle and pigs and chickens, and seen birds disappear from the skies over fields sprayed with herbicides that were meant to facilitate the growth of crops used to feed those animals. I'd put many thousands of head of cattle into confinement and seen how they suffered from unnatural conditions. I knew that while a billion people went to sleep hungry, the overfed part of the world was busy feeding sixteen pounds of grain to cattle in order to make one pound of beef. I'd seen countless friends suffer from heart attacks or require heart surgery. I'd seen the cancer rate in America increase dramatically. My own health was hardly exemplary: I weighed three hundred fifty pounds, my cholesterol was over 300, my blood pressure was off the charts, and I was getting nosebleeds.

And suddenly the circle came together for me. We were as a civilization making one big mistake, a mistake that was understandable because we had been raised to make it. We had been culturally indoctrinated to believe it to be not a mistake at all, but rather a normal and healthy habit. But this mistake was killing us as individuals just as it was destroying our land and our forests and our rivers. We were eating dead animals, and it wasn't working. If those animals had set out to take their revenge on us, they couldn't have done a better job.

And I became, right then and there, something I never dreamed I'd become: a vegetarian. At first I had trouble announcing the fact to others, because I honestly wasn't acquainted with any admitted vegetarians, and I feared ridicule. I knew many members of Congress who were gay, some of them openly so, but I didn't know any who were vegetarian. I did know one aging hippie woman from Montana who was vegetarian, but her name was Atlantis. Most folks back home in Montana would rather be caught riding someone else's horse than be accused of vegetarianism. I had always been more or less a macho kind of guy, and vegetarian just wasn't how I saw myself.

Within a year of eating no meat, my health problems all started to go away. Not only did I feel better physically, but I felt better knowing that there was one answer to many of the different ills afflicting both ourselves and our environment.

Everything revolved around the fork.

CHAPTER FIVE

# Mad Cows and Bureaucrats

In 1989, while working as a lobbyist for the National Farmers Union, I was waiting for a deadly dull meeting to start at the American Farm Bureau Federation when a representative of the National Cattlemen's Beef Association mentioned something that caught my attention. He said he had just returned from England, where he had witnessed a growing number of cattle that were presenting strange symptoms of disease. They were staggering around as if they were drunk. They were becoming extremely belligerent. And then they were dropping dead. He said the Brits were calling it Mad Cow disease. The cattlemen's rep told me all this with a slight smile, almost enjoying the plight of the unfortunate British ranchers. He said it was a good thing we didn't have anything like Mad Cow disease here because it could devastate our cattle industry.

I decided I'd better look into this. I went to a lot of libraries and bookstores and found nothing on Mad Cow disease. Finally I located a newspaper article from England that identified the disease by its scientific name: bovine spongiform encephalopathy, or BSE. A few thousand cases of the disease had been confirmed in Britain by that point. It was suspected that the condition was caused by feeding the remains of scrapie-infected sheep to cows. Scrapie (so named because it makes the infected animals scrape off their wool in reaction to intense itching) is a fatal disease afflicting sheep that has a long history in Britain. The processing of sheep carcasses had apparently undergone a change in the late seventies that made it more likely for infectious agents in sheep carcasses to survive and make their way into feed supplements. The newspaper article cited British government officials who reassured the public that BSE was nothing to worry about—cows, they claimed, were "dead-end" hosts of the disease; it could not be transmitted to people. British beef was safe. The disease itself would soon die out in cattle, as a ban had been put in place on the feeding of animal protein to ruminants. Since I knew that, in the United States, government-ordered feed bans were largely charades, I was hardly reassured.

I called a lot of medical researchers who had never heard of BSE. Then I located a brain research scientist at the Albert Einstein Institute in New York who became a font of information. She told me that BSE belonged to a family of brain-wasting diseases. Other examples were scrapie in sheep and goats, transmissible encephalopathy in mink, wasting disease in deer and elk, feline spongiform encephalopathy in cats. In humans, the story was peculiar. A cannibalistic tribe of people, the Fore Highlanders, in New Guinea, were known to develop a brain-wasting disorder called kuru. Unlike other degenerative brain disorders, kuru appeared to be infectious, but the nature of the infectious agent was a mystery, and kuru victims displayed none of the expected reactions to infection, such as inflammation, fever, and increased numbers of lymph cells. (Kuru has mostly died out since the Fore gave up eating each other in the late 1950s, proving once again that, while old habits may die hard, humans are perfectly capable of changing their diets in enlightened self-interest.) The brains of kuru victims analyzed at postmortem displayed amyloid plaques, an accumulation of protein fibers common in victims both of Alzheimer's disease and of a rare, slow-progressing brain disorder, Creutzfeldt-Jakob disease, or CJD, named after two German scientists who identified the condition in 1920. CJD is a horrible disease that usually involves deterioration into blindness, dementia, and loss of motor function. Kuru and CJD were always fatal and resulted in corpses whose brains were riddled with holes, or "spongiform."

I looked into CJD, the only form of the spongiform diseases known to affect humans in the "civilized" world. I learned that while it seemed that CJD could spontaneously appear (in one person in a million), an infectious agent was also involved, but had not yet been identified. Beyond that, few scientists were willing to do research on CJD, both because the disease was rare and because none of the common solvents and heat sterilization techniques used in bacterial research would decontaminate whatever the infectious agent was that caused the disease. Pathologists, it turned out, were generally not eager to undertake postmortem examinations of patients suspected of death by CJD. When they did, in deference to the extremely infectious nature of the disease, they wore masks, goggles, gloves, boots, caps, autoclavable operating gowns, and a disposable plastic apron under the gowns. To this day, the decontamination problem hinders CJD research.

Authors Richard Rhodes, in *Deadly Feasts,* and Sheldon Rampton and John Stauber, in *Mad Cow U.S.A.,* tell the story of how the brain-wasting disease kuru of the Fore was discovered to be related to scrapie and CJD and eventually to other mammalian encephalopathies, including BSE. But those informative books were published in 1997, and back in 1989 I continued searching almost in the dark for what facts I could find.

I learned that a biochemist at the University of California, Stanley Prusiner, had developed a theory, then considered way out in left field, that the infectious agent in all these spongiform encephalopathies was not a virus but a kind of abnormal protein he called a "prion." Prusiner had begun his research after losing a patient to dementia caused by CJD. His prion theory had been influenced, directly or indirectly, by the work of two other scientists, Tikvah Alper and Carleton Gajdusek, who had speculated that the infectious agent in scrapie might lack nucleic acid (present in all viruses, and comprising the DNA thought to carry the genetic blueprint for all life), since extracts of scrapie-infected brains had retained their ability to transmit the disease after undergoing radiation treatments that normally destroy nucleic acid. Prusiner would eventually identify fifteen amino acids at one end of a protein that he believed served as the "prion protein," which he labeled PrP, of scrapie. He was then able to determine that the gene for these prions was present not only in sheep but in all mammals tested—including humans—and that prion proteins existed in both "normal" and disease-generating forms. He concluded that "the scrapie protein propagates itself by contacting normal PrP molecules and somehow causing them to unfold and flip from their usual conformation to the scrapie shape. This change initiates a cascade in which newly converted molecules change the shape of other normal PrP molecules, and so on. These events apparently occur on a membrane in the cell interior."

If he was right, Prusiner had identified a whole new form of disease agent, as unknown to the medical community as retroviruses like AIDS had been not so long ago to the general public.

Through my friend John Stauber, I learned of a researcher at the University of Wisconsin, Richard Marsh, who seemed skeptical of the claims of the British government that cows were a dead-end host of BSE. Marsh, a warm, gentle, soft-spoken man who died in 1997, told me that he had done experiments on transmissible mink encephalopathy (TME), a disorder similar to BSE. He had taken material out of the brains of mink infected with TME and injected it into the brains of two Holstein steer calves. A year and a half later, these two steers, despite seeming healthy, suddenly fell over dead. An examination of their brains revealed spongiform disease. Marsh then transferred this brain material back to mink, and seven months later, the mink died of transmissible mink encephalopathy.

Other scientific research demonstrated that scrapie, CJD, and kuru were all transmissible among species. Richard Rhodes details, for example, an experiment of the British researcher William Gordon, who injected scrapie into many different animals.

. . . *Goats and sheep were successfully infected by feeding them scrapie-infected tissue, an oral route of infection that helped explain how the disease spread in flocks and supported the idea that cannibalism spread kuru. Goats and then mice demonstrated an inverse correlation between the size of the dose and the length of the incubation period—scrapie brain, with a higher concentration of the infectious agent, produced symptoms in a shorter time than scrapie muscle, with a lower concentration of the infectious agent. (Muscle from infected animals did, however, produce disease in other animals, an ominous discovery that everyone promptly forgot. Muscle, properly sliced and packaged, is what we call meat.)*

Like Marsh, I was skeptical of the logic of the British government. Since BSE was dormant for a period of years before becoming detectable, how could the government be at all sure that infected cattle weren't widely being slaughtered and sold to consumers? And if the government believed that BSE had been caused by the feeding of the remains of scrapie-infected sheep to cows, how could it be so sure that BSE could not jump the "species barrier" and infect humans?

I couldn't help but wonder if BSE, or something very much like it, might already be present in the United States. There had never been (and still has never been) any confirmed cases of BSE in the United States. But every year about a hundred thousand cows in this country die mysteriously of what is known as Downer Cow Syndrome. These cows—like the steers in Marsh's experiment—look fine one day and drop over dead the next. I saw this happen many times on my operation in Montana, far more often in the feedlot cattle than in the grass-fed breeding cows. Since slaughterhouses don't accept animals unless they arrive alive and ambulatory, I would typically—like other feedlot operators–sell my downer cows to the renderer. And so they were undoubtedly coming back to my feedlot and others in the form of feed.

If cannibalism played a significant role in the transmission of the variety of encephalopathy known as kuru, I wondered what the implications were of feeding cows to cows. When I asked Marsh how the mink used in his experiment had been infected with encephalopathy in the first place, he said it wasn't known for sure, but that they had been fed a diet composed mainly of downer cows.

It seemed to me then, and it seems to me now, at least possible that a BSE-like disease might be one of the factors involved in Downer Cow Syndrome. The difference between the symptoms of American downer cows and British mad cows could possibly be explained by different strains of scrapie in the two countries. Cattle injected with U.S. strains of scrapie develop a neurological disorder, but their brains don't display the spongiform nature characteristic of BSE cows in Britain.

I'd hate to think that we in the States might handle the problem the way it's been handled in Great Britain. Microbiologist Richard Lacey, in *Mad Cow: The History of BSE in Britain,* reveals that the British government's approach to managing the crisis has been a sordid mixture of denial, cover-up, half-measures, wishful thinking, false assurances, and ineptitude. The earliest known cases of BSE in Britain were confirmed in 1986, but it wasn't till 1987 that the first published report about the phenomenon appeared. Over four hundred cases of mad cows were confirmed in Great Britain that year, but the actual number of cases may have been far higher, as the disease was not yet "notifiable"; that is, there was no legal imperative to notify a veterinarian when a cow fell ill from the disease.

In 1988, the British government appointed a committee chaired by Sir Richard Southwood to assess any possible risk to human health from the presence of BSE in British cattle. None of the members of the committee had any expertise in spongiform diseases. Since it was assumed that scrapie in cow feed had caused the problem, the committee recommended that a ban be placed on the feeding of animal-derived protein to ruminants, and that farmers be required to report suspected cases of BSE. The recommendations were put into effect. The only other significant step taken was to guarantee farmers who reported cases of mad cows a compensation amounting to 50 percent of the market value of the animal. Lacey, the thorn in the side of the British government throughout the mad cow crisis, explains the twisted logic behind this program:

*But why was only half the market value for a carcass paid in compensation? I think I know. If the full value were to be paid, then farmers would be encouraged to report cases, and this would have the effect of increasing the numbers recognised and the public would be aware of the real scale of the problem. Moreover, it would cost more money!*

Over two thousand confirmed cases of mad cows were reported in Great Britain in 1988.

In 1989, the Southwood Committee issued its report. Unhampered by a lack of scientific evidence for its claims, it predicted that cows would prove to be a "dead-end host" of BSE and that the chances of it spreading from cows to humans were "remote." It predicted that the disease would die out in cattle, after felling seventeen thousand to twenty thousand cows. In the meantime, the committee took the stance that "because the possibility that BSE could be transmitted orally cannot be entirely ruled out, known affected cattle should not enter the human food chain and action now undertaken ensures this."

But the only real actions undertaken up till that point were the interdict to destroy mad cows and the ban on the feeding of animal protein to ruminants. Neither action would have been cause for reassurance to an objective party. Since BSE has a long incubation period, typically not manifesting until a cow reached four or five years of age—and most cattle are slaughtered at three years—there could be no certainty that infected beef wasn't entering the human food chain. Furthermore, a feed ban would have little effect on containing the epidemic if it were transmitted "vertically," from mother to calf, as scrapie was known to be transmitted. The government dismissed this possibility—indeed this likelihood—because it could only mean that the measures it had put into effect would prove woefully inadequate.

A second, slightly dissenting report issued by another government committee in 1989 suggested two further half-measures to meet the crisis. One was the removal of certain specified bovine offals—brain, spinal cord, spleen, thymus, intestines, and tonsils—from the human food chain. No scientific evidence indicated that only these particular offals represented a risk to the human population, but they were the offals of least commercial value. The second half-measure was a recommendation that the numbers of people dying of CJD be monitored over the next twenty years. In other words, the government was proposing that the best way to determine the scope of the problem was to wait to see how many people died! A more constructive way to find out the size of the problem would naturally be to monitor the brains of cows at postmortem—a proposal that Lacey made over and over and that the British government refused to accommodate, undoubtedly because it was afraid of what it might find out.

In 1989, over seven thousand cows were confirmed with BSE.

In 1990, the House of Commons Agriculture Committee declared again that British beef was safe. Nonetheless, as the confirmed new cases of BSE doubled to over fourteen thousand in that year, twenty-six countries banned the import of British cattle and beef.

In 1991, the Ministry of Agriculture echoed the Southwood Committee in predicting that the disease would soon die out of its own accord, and that the number of cases would peak that year. Meanwhile the first indications appeared that vertical transmission of the disease had taken place. The government, however, was not persuaded by the evidence of mad cows born after the feed ban, and in any case played down the significance of the possibility of vertical transmission, saying "it would have no significance for public health." But in reality it was highly significant because it sugested that the infectious prion agent was bloodborne and could be passed from mother to calf before, or during, birth. There is blood, of course, in the meat people eat. Vertical transmission also meant the impossibility of eradicating BSE through a mere feed ban.

In a public relations campaign, the Minister of Agriculture, John Gummer, even went so far as to attempt to feed his four-year-old daughter a hamburger on television to demonstrate the safety of the product. To her credit, she refused to take a bite.

Over twenty-five thousand new cases of BSE were confirmed in 1991.

In 1992, BSE was successfully transmitted by injection to animals from seven mammalian species, including pigs and monkeys, which both share a high percentage of biological traits with humans. Although the British government denied the obvious implications of these experiments, the risk of CJD was highlighted to the meat-eating public.

Over thirty-five thousand new cases of BSE were confirmed in 1992, despite the implementation of new procedures that effectively made it more difficult to confirm cases of the disease, particularly in cows born after the 1988 feed ban. Lacey charged quite credibly that the government was attempting to rig the numbers to make the feed ban appear to be working.

In 1993, two British dairy farmers whose herds were infected with BSE died of CJD. This was particularly troubling in light of the fact that the natural incidence of CJD in the general population is about one in a million. Also, a fifteen-year-old girl developed CJD, a disease that historically tends to attack people averaging age sixty-three. Over thirty-six thousand new cases of BSE were confirmed in 1993, despite evidence of the government attempt to "massage" the numbers downward. "It was in September 1993 that farmers began to contact me because they owned youngish cattle which they confidently believed were suffering from BSE. But Ministry vets seemed to think otherwise," Lacey recalls.

In April 1994, the government reduced its compensation for infected cows by close to 20 percent, undoubtedly in the hope of generating fewer reported cases of BSE. In July of that year, the European Community placed a ban on the export of British beef carcasses, save from those rare herds that could document an absence of BSE cases over the last six years. By the end of 1994, the number of BSE cases in cows born after the feed ban had risen to well over twelve thousand, further indicating the near-certainty of vertical transmission of the disease. Many of these mad cows were traceable to mothers who had suffered from BSE.

Another twenty-five thousand cows succumbed to BSE in 1994.

By the end of 1995, the number of confirmed BSE cows born after the feed ban approached twenty-four thousand, yet the government obstinately refused to concede the existence of vertical transmission. It ignored conclusive evidence from a vertical transfer experiment in which over thirty calves born to BSE mothers, and raised under strict controls regarding exposure to contaminated feed, nonetheless developed BSE. These results led Lacey to speculate that about 10 percent of animals from infected herds carried the infection.

When two more teenagers were diagnosed as suffering from CJD in 1995, many local school officials banned beef from school meals.

Over thirty thousand more cases of mad cows were confirmed in 1995.

On March 20, 1996, the bombshell finally hit Britain. An unprecedented ten people under the age of forty-two had recently died slow, agonizing deaths from CJD. Not only were these victims far younger than those typically afflicted by CJD—averaging twenty-seven years old—and not only did none of them have a genetic predisposition to the disease, but autopsies revealed that all had contracted a new, particularly virulent strain of CJD. The government at last was forced to admit to a possible link between BSE and this new variant of CJD. Stephen Dorrell, the Secretary of State for Health, related the conclusions of the Spongiform Encephalopathy Advisory Committee to the shocked House of Commons:

> ... the Government Surveillance Unit in Edinburgh ... has identified a previously unrecognized and consistent disease pattern. A review of patients' medical histories, genetic analysis, and consideration of other possible causes have failed to explain these cases adequately. There remains no scientific proof that BSE can be transmitted to man by beef, but the Committee has concluded that the most likely explanation at present is that these cases are linked to exposure to BSE before the introduction of the specified bovine offal feed ban in 1989.

Thus, even while apparently acknowledging what it had denied for years—that eating British beef exposed humans to the danger of the fatal CJD—the government desperately clung to a pitiful source of consolation: the more-or-less desultory "specified bovine offal feed ban" of 1989. Dorrell implied that while beef in the eighties hadn't been safe, it was safe now in the nineties, despite all the evidence indicating that the infectious agent is borne in the blood of meat. And despite the clear risk to human life, the government's first priority remained the protection of the cattle industry.

The day after the announcement that effectively reversed a decade of denials by the British government of a link between BSE and CJD, ten thousand British schools dropped beef from their menus. Ireland stepped up protections at its northern border to prevent Britons from smuggling in any infected cattle. The European Union renewed an immediate and indefinite ban on British beef.

The World Health Organization agreed with the assessment linking BSE to CJD. It concluded that a new variant of CJD existed, best explained by the consumption of beef products from mad cows. The most startling feature of the new variant was discoverable at autopsy. The brain pathology of those who succumbed was strikingly reminiscent of that of the victims of kuru in New Guinea.

In October of 1996, Dr. John Collinge reported in the British journal *Nature* on the development of a new biochemical test for prions. Using this test, Collinge determined that the biochemical "fingerprints" of prions in patients with CJD were identical to those of prions from laboratory animals infected with BSE. In an article in *Nature* a year later, the same researcher proved the link conclusively. Three samples of brain tissue were taken from patients who had died of the new variant CJD and were injected into mice. Six samples were taken from the brains of people who died from classic CJD, and injected into other mice. The mice receiving the new variant CJD all developed the same "BSE signature" as other mice injected either with brain tissue from mad cows directly or from other animals infected by brain tissue from mad cows. The mice infected with classic CJD brain tissue did not develop the "BSE signature."

Debate still continues in the scientific community about whether the spongiform encephalopathies are caused solely by aberrant prions, as Prusiner contends, or whether some virus or other substance acting as a co-factor accompanies the rogue prions. But in the same first week of October 1997 that the conclusive *Nature* article came out, Prusiner's prion theories were given a ringing endorsement when he was awarded a Nobel Prize in medicine for his research.

So far eighty-eight people in the United Kingdom have died from the new variant of CJD. It is estimated that at least 750,000 cattle infected with Mad Cow disease have entered the human food chain since the start of the epidemic. Some 350,000 tons of meat, bonemeal, and tallow suspected of contamination with BSE lie in cold storage in Britain, awaiting construction of incineration plants to deal with the mountain of offal. Nearly five million cows in Britain have been destroyed in the as-yet-unsuccessful attempt to stem the epidemic.

The panic that afflicted Britain in the late nineties is spreading, as the new millennium begins, to all of Europe. Many hundreds of cases of BSE have been uncovered in Ireland, France, Switzerland, and Portugal. Other cases have come to light in Spain, Germany, Belgium, Denmark, and Holland. Three people in France and one person in Ireland have perished from new variant CJD. On January 5, 2001, Australia and New Zealand announced a total ban on the import of beef products from thirty European countries.

The incubation period of the spongiform diseases appears to vary in direct relation to a species' natural life expectancy. Mice can incubate the disease in just a few months. It takes cats a few years from being infected to display symptoms of disease. The incubation period in humans of CJD is thought to be from ten to thirty years. Therefore the cases of CJD that have arisen in the first half of the 1990s could well have derived from the eating of infected beef in the early or mid-eighties, before BSE was even diagnosed. If so, these first deaths could prove reminiscent of the curiosity of the first handful of people who died of AIDS in the early 1980s, before the numbers of mortalities exploded and the disease spread worldwide. And the risk factors for CJD involve a greater percentage of the population than the risk factors for AIDS. They are the eating of beef and possibly (though less likely) the consumption of milk and dairy products.

There is currently no treatment for CJD, and no test for its presence other than a biopsy of brain material, usually conducted at postmortem.

If it turns out that CJD can be transmitted from mother to child in humans, as BSE is undoubtedly transmitted in cows, then the very real and frightening danger exists not only of an epidemic but of a disease that will become endemic in humans, passed on from one generation to the next. Unfortunately, there is already some evidence for this possibility. A report in the *New England Journal of Medicine* told of a thirty-nine-year-old pregnant mother in Japan who was in the thirtieth week of her pregnancy and showing signs of CJD. She delivered an apparently healthy baby by caesarean section. Material from the placenta and umbilical cord was injected into mice, which developed spongiform disease.

Nobody can know for sure the scale of the tragedy that may hit, since meat-eaters in Britain are effectively the subjects in one of the largest and most gruesome undertakings in the annals of science: an experiment to determine human oral susceptibility to spongiform disease. Richard Lacey, however, projects the worst-case scenario at two hundred thousand British deaths annually beginning around the year 2015.

How much safer, you may ask, are we in the States?

Although we also have a ban on British beef imports, we could better assess our risks if the government would test the brain material in a large sampling of downer cows. Unfortunately, our government, like the British, seems in no rush to uncover the truth.

In 1989, the American rendering industry came forth

with a voluntary initiative to no longer accept sheep heads at rendering plants, in order to avoid the possibility of infecting feed with scrapie. An FDA survey three years later found that fifteen of nineteen plants inspected had not implemented this voluntary ban, and six of them were using the rendered protein in cattle feed. No action was taken against these plants.

Similarly, although federal regulations forbid the inclusion of bone, bone marrow, and spinal cord in ground beef, an Agriculture Department survey in 1997 found those materials present in the ground meat it tested.

Unenforced safety regulations can do little more than lull us into a false sense of security.

In 1992, the Beyond Beef campaign, for which I served as executive director, filed a Freedom of Information Act request with the U.S. Department of Agriculture. We asked for any information on the chemical contamination of meat and any information on identified animal illnesses entering the human food chain. Early one morning, a low-level functionary led me to a room in the USDA South Building in Washington, D.C. He told me that I was not allowed to take even a pencil and paper into the room. Instead I was given a box of paper clips. I was to put a clip on any papers that I wanted copied, and they would be copied for me, subject of course to prior review by legal officers. The room was about twenty square feet and stacked from top to bottom with all kinds of absolutely useless inspectors' reports from slaughterhouses. After I spent the whole morning thumbing through the reports, the clerk announced that I had a choice of going to lunch at the same time as everyone else, or being locked in the room. It wasn't a tough call. I went to lunch. I came back in the afternoon and went through countless thousands more pieces of paper. I identified several hundred documents that might have some minor relevance to our concerns, most containing fairly innocuous information about the quantities of animals going to slaughter. But then I found one document of stunning interest. It was a hand-written field report from an inspector on a suspected case of Mad Cow disease. Unfortunately the handwriting was so hard to read that it was impossible to make out the inspector's name. I put a clip on the document, and stuck it in the middle of the stack I handed to the clerk, thinking that per-haps I had found some truly useful information in the mid-dle of this pile of crap.

After waiting several weeks, my office was notified that copies of the requested documents were available and were waiting to be paid for and picked up. I hurried back to the USDA office building. All the tedious documents quantify-ing animal carnage were there. Guess which one wasn't. I had just received a quick education in the government's view of freedom of information.

As of this book's publication, we don't know if Mad Cow disease has come to the United States. Cattle were imported from Britain to the States for breeding purposes until 1987. An effort has since been made to track and destroy those cattle imported in the years prior to the ban, as well as their offspring, but it would be naïve to expect such an effort to be thoroughly effective. The presence of Downer Cow Syndrome across America is certainly cause for concern. To date, our government has not responded to requests to step up its surveillance of downer cows, and conduct autopsies of their brains.

Numbers of CJD cases have not, to my knowledge, risen notably across the United States in recent years, but it's possible that an increase could be masked by an overlap in symptomatology between CJD and Alzheimer's disease, which is markedly on the rise. Often CJD is confused with other forms of dementia. When doctors at the Veterans Administration Medical Center in Pittsburgh autopsied fifty-four patients who died of dementia, they discovered that three of them had actually died of CJD. Since the disease historically strikes about one in a million, that's a shockingly high number. Also shockingly high is the number of CJD cases that have struck the northeastern corner of Texas in the last couple of years. Since April of 1996, eight cases of CJD have been diagnosed in this twenty-three-county area with a population of about a million. The victims ranged in age from forty-six to sixty-five, averaging fifty-seven, somewhat young for victims of classic CJD. At the rate of one death per million population normally attributable to CJD, one would expect to find just a single annual case of CJD in this region. If the recent rate of CJD mortality in northeastern Texas were to spread to the whole country, there would be about 1,500 CJD deaths per year in America.

The August 1997 mandate by the FDA to ban the feeding of ruminant protein to ruminants was an inadequate first step. Cattle are still fed the animal parts of many other species, including horses and pigs. Everything we know about spongiform diseases suggests that all mammalian species may be susceptible to them, and we know now that these diseases transmit readily across species barriers. Since there is no ban on the feeding of scrapie-infected sheep to pigs, and since a British experiment has shown that a pig injected with BSE contracted a form of transmissible encephalopathy, there is little reason to feel secure with a limited ruminant-to-ruminant feed ban. Worse, bovine blood meal has been excluded from the ban. Instead of making our cattle into full-fledged cannibals, we are now merely turning them into vampires. Spray-dried blood products, which have undergone little or no processing to remove infectivity, are used increasingly in the feed industry. Meat products that have been prepared for human consumption are also excluded from the FDA's list of substances prohibited in feed. Our feed ban comes up short as well when compared with that of the European Union, which forbids use of all mammalian meat and bonemeal in any ruminant feed. Even if our new regulation against the feeding of ruminant protein is scrupulously enforced (easier to do at the level of the large feed manufacturers than at the grassroots level of individual feedlot operators who might choose to mix bonemeal into their animals' feed), we should not settle for merely freeing our cattle from the no-holds-barred cannibalism that used to be forced upon them. Until we stop the transformation of cattle into carnivores, until we can be 100 percent sure that they are no longer consuming the blood and fecal material of their own species and the meat and bonemeal of any other animal, the risks of Mad Cow disease and a consequent human epidemic of CJD will be with us.

Are we destined to follow in the shameful footsteps of Britain?

# CHAPTER SIX

# Biotech Bullies

The insanity of the agrochemical system of food production has come crashing down on the heads of both dairy farmers and consumers in the bizarre case of recombinant bovine growth hormone (rBGH), whose intended purpose is to increase milk production in cows. In 1993, the FDA approved rBGH in the form of a drug called Posilac. rBGH is essentially a genetically engineered copy–although a less than perfect one–of a naturally occurring cow hormone. Its manufacturer, Monsanto, chooses to refer to the drug not as a growth hormone–since the company knows that a majority of consumers don't want artificial hormones in their milk–but rather as "recombinant bovine somatotropin (BST)," as it's a fair bet that most consumers wouldn't know the meaning of the term. A somatotropin is a growth hormone, and it will stubbornly remain a growth hormone no matter how many multisyllabic synonyms are applied to it.

Scientists have known for a long time that growth hormone extracted from a dead cow could be injected into a living one to stimulate additional milk production. (Beginning in the late fifties, scientists and doctors battled hypopituitary human dwarfism by reclaiming the pituitary glands of human corpses and injecting undersized children with human growth hormone. They had some success stimulating growth, but tragically the pooling of pituitary glands resulted in the spread of Creutzfeldt-Jakob disease, to which at least fourteen of the eight thousand individuals who received the growth hormone injections have succumbed. Today, a synthetic form of growth hormone is being used, which should pose no risk of CJD.) While it was impractical to reclaim the hormone from cows as they were slaughtered in slaughterhouses, genetic engineering allowed scientists in laboratories to develop a bacterium that would work 365 days a year—no union, no overtime—in the production of recombinant BGH. The breakthrough was as much economic as scientific; genetic engineering didn't really produce any new insights into how to increase milk production—it merely provided what seemed, at least to Monsanto, to be an economically feasible way to exploit existing knowledge, and to thereby boost the milk production of a cow by anywhere from 5 to 20 percent.

There's been much debate about whether or not rBGH represents a health risk to consumers. But there can be no debate about a very simple fact that renders the whole argument somewhat absurd: we have an enormous milk surplus in this country. We subsidize the price that dairy farmers receive in order to prevent the existing surplus from driving prices so low that they would go out of business. The last thing we need is a drug that aggravates the long-term problem of the overproduction of milk. Having invested hundreds of millions developing this pointless product, Monsanto has naturally fought vigorously for its acceptance and use, with seemingly little concern for the health consequences to cows or humans, or the economic consequences to farmers. The company acts as if it were promoting some great boon for humankind, but it is instead advancing a boondoggle.

The experience of John Kurtz, a well-respected dairyman from southeastern Minnesota, sheds light on some of the risks associated with the hormone. Kurtz's involvement with rBGH dates back to 1985, when he was hired by one of the chemical companies competing in the development of the product to conduct a trial of the synthetic hormone through a period of two lactations. (Cows typically have a nine-month lactation period after calving.) In order to accommodate a sufficient number of cows in each of three protocols (a control group, a "medium-level" rBGH group, and a "high-level" rBGH group), the study lasted a full three and a half years. It was closely monitored by the FDA, and Kurtz kept careful and voluminous records of the effects of the hormone on milk production and on the health of the cows.

The early news was positive. The first thing Kurtz noticed was that the product had the desired effect on the cows: they were milking more. He recorded a 17.9 percent milk production increase in the cows on rBGH (with a negligible difference between high and medium doses). But the stress of producing an unnatural amount of milk had drained fat and other body reserves from the cows. This affected their rates of calving, as only fourteen of forty cows on rBGH were able to conceive—a quite alarming result given that normal healthy cows rarely fail to rebreed. All fourteen who did conceive had multiple births—triplets or twins. To put this extraordinary fact in context, on my farm, out of perhaps twenty thousand cow births over the years, we had two sets of twins and no triplets. Multiple births are antithetical to the goal of increased milk production because cows are stressed by the requirements of carrying multiple calves. In fact, if dairy farmers could have their fantasy bovine hormone (and I wouldn't be surprised if some genetic engineer at Monsanto is working on it today), far from producing multiple offspring, it would give cows false pregnancies so that their bodies would "recycle" and produce milk without the physical trauma of delivering a fetus. The fetus drains energy and body fat from the cow, and if it turns out to be male, it has little or no value to the farmer. Bull calves are often knocked in the head with a sledgehammer by farmers, or sold for a pittance to veal operations.

The lack of public information about the multiple birthing problem undoubtedly left a lot of dairy farmers who used rBGH struggling to explain the phenomenon. As one such farm family reported in *Dairy Today,* "On the cow side, we are having twins too frequently, and even one set of triplets. . . . We're wondering if it is heat stress that lowered body condition, which may have further caused some kind of reproductive stress at the time of conception."

By the time of the second lactation in Kurtz's study, none of the cows were able to conceive, and there was a 19 percent death loss, and about a 15 percent incidence of "downed cows"–cows that could not stand up. The dead and downed cows were analyzed at the University of Minnesota. It was immediately evident that so much calcium had been drained from their skeletons for the increased milk production that "even their shoulder blades had a ripple effect like a ripple potato chip."

In summary, the increase in milk production was short-lived, and was far outweighed by the failures of the cows to breed, the loss of cows to death and weakness, and the costs of increased feed to try to help the cows keep up with the added stress. Other herds undergoing tests similar to Kurtz's experienced similar results.

After three years, all the cows in Kurtz's study had either died, or had become "downer cows" that could not stand on their own feet and had to be destroyed, or had simply failed to rebreed. If a cow fails to rebreed, its value plummets from perhaps as much as two thousand dollars to a mere three or four hundred dollars–the price to turn the cow into hamburger. Rebreeding is an absolutely integral part of the dairy business. Putting aside the issue of whether or not the use of growth hormones is cruel to the cow, it became painfully clear that it's bad business.

Kurtz compiled voluminous paperwork documenting every aspect of the cows' activity throughout the test. He boxed up all the data and sent it to the company that hired him to do the study. The materials were sent back to him. He assumed that a mistake had been made, so he again mailed the boxes of data to the company. Again the boxes were returned, and Kurtz was instructed by phone to maintain possession of the data until such time as the company felt an urge to stop by his farm and pick up the boxes.

After reading about the boomerang quality of Kurtz's boxed data, I asked myself the obvious question: Why would a chemical company pay a large sum of money for a valuable study and then refuse possession of the very materials it had paid for? I admit I was stumped by this one for a while. And then I realized that one of the questions posed by the USDA and the FDA to a company requesting approval of a new product is: *Have you given us all of the relevant data in your possession?* I have a sneaking suspicion that the chemical company for which Kurtz had contracted didn't want to have the unhappy facts in its physical possession so that it wouldn't feel obligated to hand them over to a regulatory agency.

When the dairy farmers were confronted with the fact that rBGH was overstraining and destroying their cow herds, an ingenious solution was found: Create super-cows. Feed them a diet rich in protein from animal sources—such as ground-up dead cows. And so here we arrive at the conjunction of the madness of bovine growth hormone and Mad Cow disease: the cannibalistic practices advocated by the pushers of rBGH substantially raised the risk that Mad Cow disease would come to America.

All this for the "greater good" of adding to our glut of cow's milk—which isn't good for us anyway.

More bad news hit the makers of rBGH after it reached its peak penetration of American dairy herds in 1995 and was being injected into about 10 percent of the nation's dairy cows: hot weather in southern states, normally a source of manageable stress to cows, was killing cows already punished by the milking demands of rBGH. Cows eat less in the heat, and cows that eat less cannot long sustain a regimen of rBGH. Herds in areas such as New Mexico, Texas, and Florida were suffering substantial losses. Florida, which had been a milk-exporting state before the introduction of rBGH, became a milk-importing state. Monsanto, still fighting to salvage its product, decided to target dairies in northern states and Canada. When Monsanto faced accusations in the press for attempting to bribe members of Canada's Bureau of Veterinary Drugs to approve rBGH, the resulting firestorm helped prevent the product from gaining governmental approval there.

American law is just another little nuisance to Monsanto

in its headlong drive to ram its product into the rumps of cows and down the throats of the American people. In spite of the fact that New York and many other states have statutes prohibiting veterinarians from taking direct or indirect compensation from pharmaceutical companies to promote their products, Monsanto has, according to an official with the New York Farmers Union, "underwritten joint promotional campaigns with veterinary clinics in an effort to sell farmers on rBGH." Monsanto issued vouchers for veterinary care in the amount of $150 to farmers who ordered the product. This effort of dubious legality proved a boon to veterinarians promoting Posilac, since they often reaped monetary benefits far surpassing the amount of the vouchers. As one farmer reported, "After our problems started . . . we experienced over a $3,000 vet bill. After discontinuing [r]BGH usage, our vet bill went to virtually zero."

Currently the drug is injected into only about 3 percent of the nation's dairy cows. The majority of farmers who use the drug now use it only in cows in their last cycle of lactation before the slaughterhouse. In these cows, the drug's interference with their breeding capacity becomes irrelevant. All the same, farmers are finding that the slightly elevated milk production in this last cycle of lactation is at least counterbalanced by the cost of each dose of Posilac, the cost of increased feed and antibiotics, and the reduced compensation for the cows once they are shipped off to the slaughterhouse, since the stress of added milking reduces body weight.

It is the ever-decisive bottom line that is defeating rBGH and will finally drive it off the market, probably sooner rather than later. As the politically neutral *Dow Jones News* reported: "In the end, however, economics and bad timing–not consumer opposition–have been the main factors limiting the product's appeal. Use of *Posilac*–at $5.80 a dose–drove up dairy farmers' already soaring feed costs and interfered with their traditional breeding routines."

Now we can't blame the *Dow Jones News* for addressing itself exclusively to bottom-line issues, and we'd be fools if we expected more of Monsanto. But surely government agencies such as the FDA, supposedly charged with protecting the public good, could have insisted on some research into the effects of drinking milk produced with recombinant growth hormones before allowing the product on to the market. In the decade of genetic engineering research on rBGH, not a single study was conducted on human subjects to determine the risks involved in consuming the milk of hormone-injected cows. Nonetheless, there is good reason to suppose that such risks may exist.

Inflammation of the udder, or mastitis, represents a significant health risk to rBGH-injected cows that could have serious implications for human health. The defining symptom of mastitis is the presence of pus in milk. All milk from dairy farmers must be, by law, tested by processing companies to determine what is called the "cell count"–a determination of the amount of bacterial cells in the milk. Cows injected with rBGH have significantly higher incidence of mastitis, resulting in significantly higher cell counts in their milk. This problem alone turned many farmers against rBGH. The risk to farmers of producing milk with high cell counts is compounded by the method used to transport the liquid. A sample of every farmer's milk is taken prior to loading the trucks that transport it. Often, these trucks will mix the milk from several farms in tanks as large as twelve thousand gallons. Upon arriving at the processing plant, all samples are tested. If a farmer's sample exceeds the acceptable cell count, he will not only sacrifice the revenue from his own dairy's milk, but also be responsible for the loss of revenue to all other producers whose milk was contaminated by it in the bulk tank. Instead of a paycheck, the farmer in effect receives a huge fine.

To combat mastitis and avoid such financial losses, farmers typically inject their cows with massive quantities of antibiotics. According to the regulations of the USDA, dairy farmers are required, for certain given time periods, to withhold the milk of cows treated with different antibiotics. There are about eighty such antibiotics approved for use in agriculture. Only seven of them are authorized for use in lactating cows, but the USDA routinely tests for only four of those. In order to get caught, farmers have to be stupid enough to use one of the four penicillin-family drugs that are currently being monitored. And even if caught, the punishment for a first violation generally takes the form of a stern letter of rebuke from an anonymous bureaucrat. A study of milk from grocery store shelves in the northeastern states found that 63 percent had detectable residues of antibiotics. A 1988 Illinois survey found that 58 percent of the drugs used on dairy farms were not approved for such use. The lacing of milk with antibiotics has undoubtedly increased as a direct consequence of the introduction of rBGH.

While the discovery of penicillin certainly deserves its recognition as one of the great life-saving medical breakthroughs of our century, the casual use—indeed, the profligate abuse—of antibiotics poses extraordinary risks to human and animal well-being. As has been well documented, such abuse results in the promotion of disease-causing organisms that have mutated to be resistant to antibiotics and are thus more deadly. Marc Lappé points out in his book *When Antibiotics Fail* that we are leaving ourselves "weaker than our so-called enemies." The war between antibiotics and microorganisms is a war we are losing, Lappé contends. "Modern pharmaceuticals cannot begin to keep pace with ever newer varieties of microorganisms which emerge . . . fully armed to resist the latest generation of antibiotics." When we potentially reinforce microorganisms by prescribing antibiotics to save human lives, the dilemma is troubling but understandable. When we do so on a large scale for the sole purpose of adding to our surplus of milk, we might as well just lock ourselves in a loony bin.

Increased use of antibiotics isn't the only danger associated with rBGH. Despite all the assurances of Monsanto and the FDA that rBGH merely mimics naturally occurring hormones and does not alter the nature of milk at all, the truth is that Monsanto's hormone has a different amino acid sequence than a cow's natural hormone. It could be possible that people who tolerate natural milk acceptably well may have an allergic reaction to milk produced by the introduction of rBGH, but the FDA has not investigated this as yet. While that remains a matter of speculation, it has been shown in several studies that milk-fat concentrations in rBGH-treated cows are abnormally high.

There's yet another potential risk to human health to be found in hormone-treated milk: Insulin Growth Factor 1 (IGF-1), a chemical in the body that controls the cellular response to growth hormone and takes exactly the same form in cows as it does in humans. An excess of IGF-1 in humans can bring about acromegaly, a disease whose symptoms include enlargement of the hands, feet, nose, and chin. Milk from cows injected with rBGH has been definitively demonstrated to possess an elevated level of IGF-1, although the degree of elevation remains in dispute, due to difficulties involved in measuring the substance. Estimates of the increase in the IGF-1 levels of the milk of rBGH-treated cows range in scientific studies from a statistically significant 25 percent to an off-the-charts 360 percent. Similar increases in IGF-1 are also found in the meat of rBGH-treated cows. Since 1994, Monsanto has publicly denied a differential in the concentration of IGF-1 in rBGH-treated cows, but in its 1993 application to the British government for permission to sell the product there, it acknowledged a 500 percent elevation in IGF-1 levels. IGF-1 is not deactivated by the processes of pasteurization or digestion, as Monsanto had claimed early in the process of stampeding its way to government approval. The growth factor ends up in the human bloodstream. What it does at that point is unknown, but some scientists suspect that it may play a role in the causation of cancer.

A study of the effect of IGF-1 on the growth of rats found a significant increase in the body weight of male rats given a high dose of the growth factor. The FDA discounted this increase in body weight for such dubious reasons as the fact that it was seen only in male and not female rats. Even in male rats fed a low dose of the hormone, kidney and liver weight increased significantly, and yet the FDA, which one would think might be alarmed by such information, chose to look away. The study, not coincidentally, was sponsored by Monsanto. Critics of the study warned that the evidence showed that "IGF-1 stimulates growth and division of epidermal cells in the intestine and has also been associated with colon tumor growth and, potentially, with human epidermal carcinoma," adding that "until we know more about the role of IGF-1, extreme caution should be exercised." The critics were not heeded; the study was not repeated.

Different scientific studies have implicated insulin growth factors in colorectal, thyroid, bone, and breast cancers. Researcher Robert Cohen synopsized the cancer risk attendant upon the use of rBGH this way:

> *Armed with the knowledge that virtually all humans have tumors waiting to proliferate, and [that] milk hormones (IGFs) cause proliferation of cancer, and that treatment of cows with recombinant bovine growth hormone causes an increase in IGF levels in milk, it is now time for science, industry and FDA to re-investigate and re-evaluate this controversy.*
>
> *It is also appropriate that FDA immediately place a moratorium on the use of rBST until appropriate testing can be completed.*

All of these legitimate health concerns have persuaded the fourteen-member European Union as well as Canada to place a moratorium on the use of rBGH.

One would think that, given the considerable controversy regarding the safety of a major food product, at least part of the solution would involve allowing consumers to decide for themselves. By simply requiring the labeling of milk that was produced with recombinant bovine growth hormone, the government could ensure that consumers had the chance to vote with their pocketbooks. The trouble, from Monsanto's standpoint, was that surveys clearly showed that approximately three-quarters of consumers expressed concerns about possible negative long-term effects on their health from genetically engineered milk. Even though labeling of dairy products from rBGH-treated cows was favored in various surveys by 80 to 98 percent of consumers, the FDA and Monsanto realized that labeling would be the kiss of death for the product they both had grown to care so much about. It's hard to believe it was only a coincidence that milk sales throughout the nation dropped dramatically in the month that rBGH was approved for use. Many retail stores around the nation—including such hardly radical elements as 7-Eleven stores, and Pathmark, ShopRite, and Kroger supermarkets—expressed interest in trying to avoid selling genetically engineered milk to their customers. They could not effectively do so, however, in the absence of labeling. The FDA stubbornly held to its untenable position that milk produced from rBGH-treated cows was "virtually" indistinguishable from milk from normal cows, and therefore that mandatory labeling of rBGH milk was unnecessary. The FDA further supported Monsanto by insisting that, should any milk producer engaged in interstate commerce (over which the FDA has jurisdiction) wish to voluntarily label its products as being free of artificial hormones, it might do so only if it added that "No significant difference has been shown" between milk derived from treated and untreated cows. It would also be required to keep extensive records on each cow involved in its production, participate in a "third party certification program," and await inspection on demand. Thus when genetically engineered cow's milk came onto the market for human consumption, the long arm of government protection swept down to insist on a stringent set of protocols—not for the farmers using the controversial new technology, but for those openly doing things the old-fashioned way.

The good people of Vermont have a long tradition in the dairy business, and much of it is oriented to family farming. They have a free and independent spirit—even their present congressman is an Independent—and to them Posilac was a skunk in the henhouse. They believed that milk produced with artificial hormones and not labeled as such represented a direct insult to their rights as producers and consumers of the product in its traditional form. In 1994, Vermont became the first state in the nation to mandate labeling for dairy products from cows injected with rBGH. Before you could say *spilt milk*, the International Dairy Foods Association, undoubtedly acting at the behest of Monsanto, took the state of Vermont to court. According to the lawsuit, the "mandatory labeling of milk products derived from supplemented cows will have the inherent effect of causing consumers to believe that such products are different from and inferior to milk products from unsupplemented cows."

Consider for a moment the mind-boggling logic behind this complaint. It amounted to this: *We say there's no difference between our genetically engineered milk and regular milk, therefore consumers have no right to know which is which.* Obviously they had reason to fear the choice that informed consumers would make. But the American system of capitalism, in my reading of it, involves free access both to products and to information consumers need and want in order to make their buying choices. Then the market dictates a product's success. Remember how Willow Jeane told me I could make the big decisions, as long as she got to make the little decisions—such as deciding which decisions were which? Well, here's Monsanto teaming up with our government to tell us we can make the big decision of choosing our milk, as long as they get to make the little decision to not let us know what's in it.

Monsanto sent threatening letters widely to milk retailers warning them that they could be violating federal law by advertising that they were selling milk that came from cows free of rBGH. The $7.7 billion multinational even went to the length of suing a small, family-owned dairy in Waco, Texas, and a cooperative of family-owned dairies in Iowa that proclaimed their milk free of the artificial hormone. Monsanto's tactics of intimidation were not surprising. Our ire ought to be raised, however, by the fact that the agency ostensibly charged with serving the citizenry, the Food and Drug Administration, instead of safeguarding our right to know, worked behind the scenes with Monsanto to negate it.

Why would the FDA go out of its way to protect Monsanto's interests? It's interesting to note that three top-level officials of the FDA involved in formulating the drug agency's positions on the synthetic hormone had previously been paid by Monsanto either for legal work or scientific studies of rBGH. When Congressmen David R. Obey of Wisconsin, George E. Brown of California, and Bernard Sanders of Vermont pressured the General Accounting Office for a review of these ethically dubious circumstances, they received a whitewash report denying that any conflict of interest existed. One of the three bureaucrats concerned has now returned to his position as a partner in the Washington law firm of King and Spalding, which represents Monsanto. We can only speculate why a high-earning attorney would take a significant pay cut for a period of years to work for a government agency while it decided the fate of a former client's product, then return to private practice and representation of that client once the issue was favorably resolved. Maybe he just felt patriotic there for a spell.

The state of Vermont won the first round against Monsanto's lackeys, when a U.S. District Court judge upheld the state's right to require truthful labeling of dairy products. On appeal, however, a Circuit Court panel sided with the plaintiffs, and suspended the state law. That is how the matter rests today. No state in the nation has a standing law mandating labeling of milk products to let consumers know whether or not those products were genetically engineered. Nonetheless, on August 15, 1997, consumers won a victory that may have turned the tide decisively against the biotech lobby on the issue of rBGH. Ben & Jerry's, the manufacturer of ice cream and frozen yogurt based in Monsanto's nemesis state of Vermont, joined by Stonyfield Farm, Whole Foods Market, and Organic Valley foods, reached a settlement with the state of Illinois that will allow the food producers to say on the labels of their dairy products that they are rBGH-free. They had sued on the grounds that any prohibition of voluntary anti-rBGH labeling violated their First Amendment rights to provide honest information to their customers.

The settlement should ease the dilemma faced by retailers, who had been "caught between a rock and a hard place," as Ronnie Cummins, the director of the nonprofit Pure Food Campaign, explains:

*They know that consumers, parents, and family dairy farmers want "rBGH-free" milk and dairy products. They know that people want "rBGH-free" foods labeled or advertised as such, and they know that these products will likely outsell suspect brands. On the other hand they are afraid of Monsanto and their own state agricultural officials, who are invariably pro-biotech.*

Despite all the power players in Monsanto's corner, it's clear that Posilac will not be with us for too long, since the product simply causes more economic losses than gains for farmers. It's hard to believe that Monsanto didn't realize this early on. What was the company thinking as it continued to pursue this monumental boondoggle, which has been estimated by financial analysts to be costing Monsanto $10 million a year?

Well, it knew it was a safe bet that, given the hype, the product would be picked up by a certain percentage of innovative farmers, and would cause at least a short-term increase in milk production. If Monsanto could merely instill the fear into farmers that their competitors were going to achieve a 15 to 20 percent increase in milk production, and a proportionate increase in income, then those farmers would feel that they had no choice but to embrace the new technology. The only part of the income equation that farmers control, after all, is production, and, given a choice, they generally do all they reasonably can do to increase it. The only scenario that could derail Monsanto's plan was an absolute production disaster—and that is exactly what has come to pass. In agriculture, news travels fast, and bad news at the speed of light, and so Monsanto has been thrown up against the wall sooner than it might have guessed.

Posilac was designed to be used in herds that had a very sophisticated management system—a system in which herd health was secondary to production targets. Since family farmers have traditionally placed more emphasis on herd health and contented cows than they have on bottom-line results, Monsanto targeted its efforts from the beginning toward factory dairies. Not only could they sell more doses of the drug to the large dairy operations, but those farmers were already accustomed—as I had once been—to working closely with veterinarians on a whole host of health problems arising from the unnatural diet and confinement of their cattles, and had less reason to fear a product injurious to cow health. Large factory dairies typically cull their cows young from the herd, sending them off to become hamburger after only one or two lactations, at about four years of age. On family farms, cows are more likely to live six to twelve years. Even if small dairies had the will to embrace a biotech product, they lacked the necessary capital, expertise, labor, and veterinary support. Thus Posilac was a product that couldn't have been better designed to pit the factory farm against the family farm. As soon as the product was introduced, milk production went up, domestic consumption dropped, the glut of milk increased, milk prices fell, and consumer confidence plummeted. The combination of those events sealed the fate of many family farmers, aggravating the ominous decline of a proud American tradition. Currently, we're losing about a hundred thousand family farms a year. Synthetic growth hormone has helped to speed up the process.

Let's take one final look at all genetically engineered milk has to offer us. Here's a product that makes cows produce more milk than they're naturally equipped to give, and that as a result destroys the physical condition of the animals, interfering with their breeding cycles when it doesn't destroy them outright, and that also causes infections of their udders, which in turn compels farmers to increase their use of antibiotics, aggravating an unhealthy dynamic whose ultimate result will be enhanced enemy microorganisms. The milk produced by the implementation of this engineering miracle contains elevated levels of a growth hormone implicated in a variety of cancers and other diseases. The costs of using the product are significant, starting with the costs of the drug itself, then adding to that the costs of the labor involved in injecting it and the extra feed needed to help the cows sustain the unnatural burden on their systems, and the veterinary costs that are so inevitably linked to the product's use that the manufacturer included vet vouchers as a sales tool to help offset that expense. The recommended feed to help cows survive the demands of the product is animal protein, which raises the specter that the product's use could advance the spread of Mad Cow disease. By appealing exclusively to large dairy herds, the product threatens to pit the large farmer against the family farmer. To the extent that it works as advertised and helps farmers produce more milk, it will only add to a chronic oversupply and help depress milk prices further, thereby throwing more family dairy farmers out of business. And by reducing consumer confidence in the safety of milk, it limits demand for milk as well as other dairy products, again depressing prices and threatening the livelihood of the small farmer.

It's time to put this genie back in its bottle.

# Chapter Seven

# Bovine Planet

Most new vegetarians soon enough learn the first question that they repeatedly will have to field: *Why do you abstain from meat—for health or for moral reasons?* Having raised for slaughter an untold number of cattle myself, I wouldn't presume to tell anyone whether it's inherently wrong to kill an animal for food. It's obviously a question people can answer only from their gut; there is no absolute right and wrong that can be ordained from on high or logically deduced by philosophical reasoning, since the value of the life of a farm animal may be highly significant to one person, and thoroughly insignificant to another. Some believe that it's wrong to make animals suffer; others question whether animal suffering has any meaning or importance, or believe it justified by the greater "good" of providing food to humans. Some get queasy at the thought of slaughtering a cow or a pig or a chicken; others, currently the majority, obviously don't—or else manage to eat these animals quite happily without thinking about what their dinner was before it became meat. Still others, while having no qualms about a fundamental human privilege to consume animals, object if those animals are raised on factory farms in cruel and unhealthy conditions; these people seek out "free-range" beef and chicken and probably have a hell of a time ordering meat in restaurants. I for one don't expect the inherent moral issues regarding the right of human beings to kill and consume "lower" life forms to ever be fully resolved—any more than I expect a consensus to suddenly be reached on the matter of abortion. There is in both cases the impossibility of deciding on the value of a form of life (whether an animal or a human fetus) that cannot express itself and that may or may not possess what we generally think of as "consciousness." I am not given to moralizing on issues so murky, although I've got to confess that sometimes, when listening to "pro-life" advocates condemn abortion with a tone of absolute moral certainty, I wonder whether or not they eat meat.

There is, however, a moral basis for the vegetarian diet for which the indeterminate value of an animal's life takes on irrelevance. And that moral basis is a concern for the environment, a value as absolute as the value we all place on *human* life, since humanity will not long survive on a poisoned planet. To be an environmentalist who happens to eat meat is like being a philanthropist who doesn't happen to give to charity.

As we do with thoughts of our own mortality, we tend to respond to predictions of looming environmental disaster by putting the matter out of our mind. We may label as "alarmist" someone who contends that our global pattern of environmental abuse will threaten civilization as we know it within, say, thirty years; but, in the long run, what difference does it make if the "alarmist" is right in his diagnosis of the problem but wrong in the timing of his particular doomsday by twenty or fifty or a hundred years? Would we be satisfied to inhabit a planet that is livable for only another century or so? Satisfied if our children or grandchildren are the last generations to live out reasonably normal lives before environmental conditions become globally unbearable?

Already we are seeing forests, lakes, rivers, shorelines, and coral reefs die, fish and sea mammals disappear from our waters, birds disappear from our skies, frogs and other amphibians threatened, arable land decline in quantity and quality, and global food production per capita decline. We are losing precious rain forest at the rate of 2.4 acres per second. How much more destruction will we need to observe before we begin to make the protection of the Earth a greater human priority than our international competitions in commerce and armaments?

I often hear politicians pontificate about the immorality of leaving our growing national debt to our children and grandchildren. They are positively outraged; you can practically see the blood vessels bursting in their faces as they deplore the injustice of it all. Often they recommend a change in our Constitution as the remedy. Well, wrong though it may be to burden our progeny with debt, I guarantee you that our descendants would rather contend with some inherited fiscal debt than dead rivers and oceans, spreading deserts, unproductive soil, depleted energy reserves, lost forests, and foul air.

It is, of course, imperative that we understand the nature and causes of ecological destruction in order to stop it. But in facing these causes of unimaginable blight, we have to have the guts and the integrity to look at our own habits, and in particular, to the fork.

In his book *Agricide,* Dr. Michael W. Fox sums up the effects of animal agriculture this way: "An estimated eighty-five percent of all U.S. agricultural land is used in the production of animal foods, which in turn is linked with deforestation, destruction of wildlife species, extinction of species, loss of soil productivity through mineral depletion and erosion, water pollution and depletion, overgrazing, and desertification." When we dare to think of the environmental threats facing our planet, we must indeed consider a complex web of interrelated problems: air pollution, water pollution, land contamination, soil erosion, wildlife loss, desertification (the turning of verdant land into a condition resembling natural desert), rain forest destruction, and global warming. Humankind's profligate consumption of animal products has made a significant contribution to all of these ills, and it stands as the leading cause of many of them. Certainly these problems wouldn't disappear overnight if the world suddenly became vegetarian, but no other lifestyle change could produce as positive an impact on these profound threats to our collective survival as the adoption of a plant-based diet.

You may be wondering how meat creates air pollution. After all, cows, hogs, and chickens don't have smokestacks, and the process of chopping them up shouldn't have any nefarious effect on our air.

Maybe it shouldn't, but the modern method of raising beef does harm our air quality in a myriad of ways. First and perhaps most important, there is the loss of forest and the destruction of *biomass* (the mass of living organisms) that are often required for the raising of cattle. About one-third of the annual increase of carbon dioxide in the atmosphere comes from the burning of the Earth's biomass. Much of the clearing and burning of forests is undertaken solely to make room for cattle. (I cleared 2,000 acres myself.) When plant life is burned, it's a double-whammy for the environment. Not only does the carbon contained within the trees and other plants turn into carbon dioxide but they are no longer alive to serve as Nature's air filter, making the air breathable for us by recycling carbon dioxide into oxygen through photosynthesis. Plant leaves also extract pollutants from the air. I think of the sixties' catchphrase: *If you're not part of the solution, you're part of the problem.* Well, it applies to trees, too. Living trees are a big part of the solution. Dead trees are a big part of the problem.

Second, remember that it takes roughly sixteen pounds of grain to create one pound of beef. Think of all the energy required to run the tractors, to fuel the planes that spray the crops, to power the combines that harvest them—all of this expense of energy for feed grains is ultimately dedicated to beef or pork or chicken. Eighty percent of American grain production is currently destined for the gullets of animals. As Jeremy Rifkin explains in his excellent book *Beyond Beef:*

> *It now takes the equivalent of a gallon of gasoline to produce a pound of grain-fed beef in the United States. To sustain the yearly beef requirements of an average family of four people requires the consumption of over 260 gallons of fossil fuel. When that fuel is burned it releases 2.5 tons of additional carbon dioxide into the atmosphere—as much $CO_2$ as the average car emits in six months of normal operation.*

The transportation of cattle to slaughter and the packaging and freezing of meats are energy-intensive procedures. Fruits and vegetables, by comparison, don't need to be frozen and don't need to be packaged before reaching your table—and increasingly, with the proliferation of farmers' markets, they are sold fresh, with minimal expenditures of energy. Energy is also required to control temperatures in the artificial "living" environments of animals confined to feedlots, to transport feed to animals and to transport their waste away, to manufacture and transport antibiotics and other pharmaceuticals employed in the "care" of animals in our animal factories. A study at Ohio State University comparing various types of meats with various types of plant foods found that *even the least efficient plant food is nearly ten times as efficient as the most efficient animal food.* There is almost always an unseen pollution cost to the production of energy. Lowering the energy requirements of our nutrition would thus help us reduce our dependence on foreign oil and nuclear power plants.

Third, the governmental limitations, lax though they are, on the use of pesticides for human consumption do not apply to crops destined for livestock. The lion's share of the agrochemical poisons sprayed into the air and falling onto the ground are dedicated to the production of meat.

Fourth, petrochemical fertilizers are generously employed in the production of feed grains for livestock. Nitrous oxide, one of the notorious "greenhouse gases" believed to be responsible for global warming, is emitted in the production of chemical fertilizers. On the organic dairy farm begun by my great-grandfather and carried forward by my grandfather and my father, the manure of the livestock was returned to the soil, enriching it in the way Nature intended. On the feedlot operation that I began, it would have taken far too much time and labor to return to the soil the piles of cow dung accumulating in the concrete feedlot. With the average cow producing twenty-five pounds of waste per day, and five thousand head of cattle in the feedlot, moving the waste to the soil could have easily occupied two workers around the clock, costing $50,000 to $100,000 a year in labor. To save that cost, we simply created mountains of waste inside and outside the feedlot. As a result, we had to spray the feedlot constantly to fight the flies that were attracted to the manure, and we had to pour chemical fertilizer into the impoverished soil to replenish it. (In addition to the ecological cost inherent in the manufacture and transport of chemical fertilizer, there is a hidden health cost involved in their use, since fertilizer is generally composed of some mixture of only three elements—nitrogen, phosphorus, and potassium—and contains none of the trace minerals such as zinc or selenium normally present in healthy soil, whose benefits to human well-being are only now starting to be understood and documented. These trace elements are increasingly absent from foods that are not grown organically.)

Fifth, the 1.3 billion head of cattle in the world emit an estimated 150 trillion quarts of methane gas, which is the second most significant contributor (behind carbon dioxide) to the greenhouse effect. Every cow emits up to 400 quarts of methane gas daily. The chopping back of forest to make room for these prolifically gassy ungulates also makes an indirect contribution to methane pollution. When trees are simply cut and not burned, they provide wonderful food for the earth's proliferating termite population, which produces methane as a by-product of the digestion of wood. Termites are considered responsible for adding millions of tons of methane to the atmosphere annually. Scientists estimate that the methane content of the atmosphere has doubled in the last two hundred years.

Finally, the stripping of the land and desertification that are concomitants of livestock grazing result in increased dust in the air. Bared soil is lost to the wind, and the result is widespread particulate pollution, increasingly recognized as a danger to humans and a factor in trapping solar radiation and bringing about climatic changes. Dust storms have been linked to livestock grazing in Africa, the Middle East, China, Australia, and the western United States.

To be generous to the meat industry, I won't mention the pollution caused by ambulances rushing around cities to pick up heart attack and stroke victims, or the energy costs involved in their hospitalizations.

What the livestock industry does to our air, however, pales next to the extraordinary damage it does to our land and water. Cattle are as adept at destroying streams and rivers as they are at degrading land and fouling the air. Wading cows widen streams unnaturally, as their hooves break off large chunks of soil and deposit them into the water. As naturalist George Wuerthner points out, "This damage is so prevalent that most people do not realize that sluggish brown waterways were not the norm in the pristine West." As the widened, more shallow streams grow warmer by greater exposure to the sun through both greater surface area and reduced plant cover, algae proliferate, water evaporates more easily, and less dissolved oxygen is available for the fish that need it to survive. While an increase of only five degrees in water temperature can spell doom for some species of fish, the changes brought on by livestock grazing have been known to increase water temperatures by ten degrees or more. Massive "fish kills" and the demise of other aquatic animals are often the result.

While cattle hooves widen our streams and rivers, cattle dung pollutes it. Often livestock waste is dumped in streams as the most efficient means of disposal. Feedlot wastes can be several hundred times more concentrated than raw domestic sewage. Ammonia, nitrates, and bacteria generated by this waste inevitably wind up polluting rivers, streams, and wells. It is a problem of awesome dimension. On a typical feedlot, with ten thousand head, as much as half a million pounds of cow dung is produced daily. The largest feedlots, with one hundred thousand head, have a waste problem equal to that of the largest American cities. Livestock waste exceeds human waste in tonnage nationwide by a factor of one hundred and thirty! It's been estimated that animal wastes are responsible for ten times as much water pollution in America as the human population. Moreover, every year thousands of cattle carcasses are left to rot in streams and rivers, polluting them further.

Perhaps the most dramatic story of what the livestock industry can do to our water, and what that poisoned water can do to us, is told in Rodney Barker's compelling book *And the Waters Turned to Blood*. It is a powerful story, as frightening as it is fantastic.

Dr. JoAnn Burkholder, a research scientist and professor in the field of aquatic botany at the University of North Carolina, became an expert on a previously unknown single-cell organism named *Pfiesteria piscicida*. Burkholder's research on *Pfiesteria* revealed how remarkably amorphous and insidious a creature it could be. First by the thousands, and then by the millions, fish were turning up dead in the waters of North Carolina—the result, Burkholder proved, of the proliferation of *Pfiesteria,* which emits a deadly toxin. Many of these fish had open sores. More frightening still, fishermen and vacationers who had had exposure to the rivers and estuaries of North Carolina where the massive fish kills were taking place were developing body sores, acute losses of memory, strange bouts of temper, and seizures. What caused *Pfiesteria* suddenly to proliferate and make itself a genocidal threat to fish and a considerable threat to the human population? There may have been many causes, but one loomed larger than the others.

Pork.

*Pfiesteria,* you see, thrives in nutrient-rich waters. Nutrient pollution has many causes. It may be caused by runoffs of urban sewage. It may be caused by runoffs of pesticides and of nitrogen and phosphorus used in fertilizers. And increasingly it is caused by the waste of factory farms. Over the decade preceding the emergence of *Pfiesteria,* North Carolina had risen, largely by dint of the laxity of its environmental regulations, to the dubious honor of being the number-two state in hog production in America, behind only Iowa—a state in which the awful stench of hog operations has made life unlivable for so many of its citizens that reining in the hog operators became a hot issue in the state's 1996 presidential caucuses.

Ruptures of swine lagoons turned rivers brown and brought about the massive fish kills in the waterways of North Carolina. Fecal coliform bacteria in the New River was discovered to exceed state standards by a factor of thirty thousand. The state of North Carolina, fearing an impact on its tourist industry, and unwilling to confront its hog industry, for a long time attributed the fish kills to low levels of dissolved oxygen—a naturally recurring phenomenon. In a way reminiscent of the British government denying the truth about Mad Cow disease to protect its cattle industry, the state of North Carolina sought to suppress the truth about fish kills and the illnesses of its own citizens in the interest, mainly, of its hog operators. But when fish kills reached into the millions, and the majority of dead fish revealed the open bleeding wounds characteristic of *Pfiesteria* feasting, while at the same time levels of dissolved oxygen in the afflicted waterways remained sufficient to support aquatic life, the truth became evident to the people of the state, and Burkholder's views were vindicated.

*Pfiesteria* has since been found in waters from Delaware Bay to the Gulf of Mexico. In August and September of 1997, thousands of fish on the tributaries of Chesapeake Bay developed the raw, gaping sores that are the fingerprint of *Pfiesteria*. Governor Parris N. Glendening of Maryland was forced to close stretches of several rivers. What was the suspected cause of the outbreak? Chicken manure, from chicken farms and from cornfields where the manure is spread and drained by ditches into streams.

Thanks to animal agriculture as it's currently practiced, *Pfiesteria* may be coming soon to a waterway near you. If it isn't already there.

Humanity's water dilemma has two dimensions: pollution and usage. Dreadful though it always is to pollute a river or a well or a freshwater stream, the harm is amplified in direct proportion to the degree of need that the human community feels for that resource. If we could limit our need for water, we would be able to devote more attention to ensuring the quality of the water we use. Keep that fact in mind as I tell you this: *the meat industry is draining this country dry.* Author Lynn Jacobs recounts the facts in his definitive book *Waste of the West:*

> *In the Northwest, livestock production accounts for over half the water consumed in the entire region. Half of Arizona's water use is for livestock. . . . Most of California's share of*

*Colorado River water doesn't get to Los Angeles swimming*
*pools but to irrigated pastures and cropland for cattle; over-*
*all, stockmen account for well over half of the state's water*
*use. A recent federal hearings report on subsidized irrigation*
*stated that 97.5% of Montana's water use was for some form*
*of livestock production. . . .*

All in all, about 70 percent of the water used in the eleven western states is dedicated to the raising of animals for food. Yet ranchers have not stopped at merely diverting the flow of rivers and tapping our priceless aquifers; they have also drained marshes, swamps, and ponds, destroying ecologically valuable wetlands for the short-term benefit of their cattle.

We often hear about water shortages in areas such as Southern California, where citizens are recurrently requested not to wash their cars, not to overwater their lawns, and to use low-flow showers and toilets. Good ideas, all. But you never hear city, county, or state governments combating drought by urging their citizens to cut down on meat consumption, even though the water required to produce *just ten pounds of steak* equals the water consumption of the average household for a year. (Of course, the water saved by a sudden reduction in meat consumption would not produce an immediate savings in water needed by a given drought-stricken community, but I make the point to give some perspective to the water problem and to illustrate where our long-term, global priorities need to be focused.)

America was blessed with the largest underground lake in the world—the Ogallala Aquifer. It took millions of years of seeping rainwater to create the Ogallala, which reaches from Texas to South Dakota, from Missouri to Colorado—

and we are depleting this resource at a rapid rate. Nearly half the grain-fed cattle in America are raised by farmers dependent upon the Ogallala to irrigate their crops. Over the last four decades, an average of about three cubic miles of water has been drained annually from this reserve. Wells are already running dry across northern Texas, and in the coming decades much of the irrigated land of the Great Plains states may well return to desert conditions. On stretches of land at the fringes of the Ogallala in Missouri, Colorado, and Nebraska, the cost of irrigation has made farming no longer economically feasible, and land that in the immediate past was green and lush and productive today is blowing in the wind, abandoned by chemical farmers. At the current rate of usage, the great Ogallala will be mostly exhausted within the next half-century.

Much of the water that livestock producers are not taking from a precious resource like the Ogallala they are taking from you and me—the taxpayer. Our tax dollars have paid for more than half the costs of irrigation projects in the United States this century. The average cost to the government of subsidized irrigation is fifty-four dollars an acre. The benefits go to a smaller and smaller number of agribusinesses.

*Well,* you may say, *so much for grain-fed beef.* Clearly the environmental and energy costs of growing sixteen pounds of grain to get one pound of beef are luxuries humanity can no longer afford. But what about steers that are fed more naturally on grass, not grain, and are raised on ranches and public land? Doesn't this way of making steak take less of a toll on the environment?

Not by a long shot. Ranch-raised beef is probably even more environmentally destructive than feedlot beef, though from the Earth's point of view, that's a little like comparing Hitler to Stalin.

The biological productivity of the western range has been estimated to have been reduced, since the introduction of grazing, by some 90 percent. In the case of ranching on public lands in the West, the trade-off between the cost to the environment and the "gain" of the meat produced as a consequence practically defies the imagination. Public lands ranching, as we will see, results in extraordinary destruction of native vegetation and wildlife, causes widespread flooding, soil erosion, and water pollution, costs the American treasury $1 billion or more annually—and produces only 3 percent of American beef! In short, if we were to shut down tomorrow the entire industry of ranching on public lands, we probably wouldn't even notice the difference in terms of the supply—or price—of beef, but we *would* notice something else: slowly but surely, much of the western United States would begin to turn from brown to green, and its rivers would begin to run clean again (at least in areas secure from feedlots). The smell of dung would be replaced by the smells of native grasses and flowers, the air would become cleaner, and the land would again belong to the people and to all wildlife, not just to the bovine usurpers.

As Lynn Jacobs writes: "Ranching has wasted and is wasting the Western United States more than any other human endeavor." Those of us who have traveled in virtually any area of the West can attest to the truth of that statement. I recall driving in northern Montana during one of our frequent dry spells and seeing the range stripped so clean a gopher would have to pack a lunch. You could see the cow pies on the range a half mile away. The grass was gone, the trees were bare, the streams were dry, and the banks of the streams were flattened by the foraging of cows. The country was so denuded that the deer were forced to browse in the fenced-off ditches along the side of the highway–the only place grass grew beyond the reach of cows. What had once been a rich grassland had been transformed into a moonscape.

For a long time now, men who have been romanticized as cowboys have cast a greedy eye on the grasslands of the West, seeing the green not so much of grass as of money. I used to be one of them, more or less–the modern kind, who brought many of his cows indoors. But I can tell you that when I looked at grassland adjacent to my farm, I saw its potential to fatten up my cows for slaughter. This rapacious attitude has endured since the white man came to America, and unfortunately the environmental devastation we cowboys have wreaked has been cumulative.

With the invention of barbed wire in 1874, stockmen were able to mark off their territory and divvy up public lands. By bringing up to forty million cattle and fifty million sheep onto the western range in the last decades of the nineteenth century, ranchers denuded vast areas of land. All told, some seven hundred million acres of grassland were stripped bare.

A cowboy reign over the western half of the United States that began in the nineteenth century with violence and terror, marauding livestock and murder, illegal land grabs and intimidation of public officials, bribery, theft, and giveaways of federal land, continues today in a more decorous way with political action committees and lobbyists for powerful ranching interests. Sparsely populated western states like my own Montana benefit as well from the Constitution, which gives them as much representation in the United States

Senate as such heavily populated states as New York. Often, the most influential political forces in the more lightly populated western states are ranching empires—empires that are sometimes headed by the descendants of those who stole and cheated their way onto "their" land in the first place. These ranching interests do not lobby for the good of the western range, for the land or the water or the air or even for the people who live upon it. They lobby for their own short-term profits, and they have a history of doing so with almost unbroken success. The thousand or so ranchers who graze their cattle on public land in Arizona, for instance, have far more say in that state's land-use policies than its other 3.7 million residents combined.

Few people realize that it was the taste for beef and the grazing industry that fed it that, more than anything else, virtually wiped out the Native Americans throughout this continent. The competition for land that lay behind the violence between "cowboys and Indians" was made necessary only because the cowboys required vast stretches of grassland for their cattle. In addition, livestock depleted the vegetation and supplanted the animals around which Native Americans had built their cultures.

Powerful stockmen allied to induce Congress in 1905 to set up the United States Forest Service, and to place it under the jurisdiction of the business-oriented U.S. Department of Agriculture, rather than the Department of the Interior, which is historically at least a bit more sensitive to issues of conservation of resources. To this day, at taxpayer expense, the Forest Service administers grazing rights on public lands, and sells those rights for nominal fees, usually considerably lower than the fees for comparable private lands. In fact, federal agencies typically spend more money to administer grazing allotments than is returned to the Treasury in fees. The government often picks up the tab for water pipelines, fences, cattle guards, seeding, and weeding. The government's Animal Damage Control division kills an estimated 250,000 wild animals annually to accommodate the ranchers who don't want them harming their livestock. The government also transfers public grazing leases when ranches dependent on those leases change hands; these leases therefore enhance the value of private property, only adding to the wealth of those most interested in protecting the "right" to graze public land. The politics of public grazing, a classic example of the wealthy and powerful feeding at the public trough, make public lands ranching appear unassailable. Meanwhile, the consequent ecological damage to the Western half of the United States has continued virtually unabated for more than a century.

Many cattlemen today, contrary to myth, are essentially Gucci-booted business executives who have often inherited their wealth and power. They do not mind at all that when their fellow citizens think of cowboys, they think of noble, rugged, independent, self-starting men—not the usurpers of federal property who have continued the rapacious land-use practices that helped bring about, among other ecological catastrophes, the Dust Bowl disaster of the 1930s. As journalist Richard Lessner of *The Arizona Republic* expressed it, "The hard truth is that we don't need the West's cattle ranches anymore. They're as much a historical oddity as the steam locomotive and the whalebone corset. The ranchers just haven't realized it yet."

I've had a lot of friends who considered themselves cowboys. I've been a cowboy myself. I've got nothing against rugged independence as a character trait. I just think it's time we disabused ourselves of the romantic image of the cowboy and took a hard look at the reality of what the cattle culture has done to our land.

Almost all public lands ranching in America takes place in the eleven western states, and virtually all land in those states that can possibly be grazed by livestock is currently being used for that purpose. Seventy-five percent of the 418 million acres of publicly owned land in the West (federal, state, and local) is used by ranchers for private gain. Two government agencies–the Bureau of Land Management (BLM) and the Forest Service–administer 85 percent of public ranchland, ranging from National Forests to grasslands to brushlands, shrublands, and riparian areas. While raising beef is always an inherently inefficient business, doing so on public land in the arid West takes the grand prize for wastefulness. Consider that in Iowa, for instance, a cow needs to graze one acre per year to survive and fatten. The average Alabama cow requires three acres per year. By contrast, on western land controlled by the BLM and the Forest Service, a cow needs to graze no less than one hundred and eighty-five acres per year at public expense to fatten equivalently!

In 1975, the BLM issued a report on the condition of the land under its management, and concluded that 83 percent of its rangeland was in an unsatisfactory state. That report was criticized by the General Accounting Office for *understating* the deteriorating condition of the lands controlled by the BLM.

The average range steer consumes six tons of range plant material before going to slaughter. Vegetation and seeds that are not consumed by cattle are often killed by the trampling of livestock hooves. An untold number of plant species have been wiped out by overgrazing, and often the "invad-ing" plants that have replaced them by virtue of being un-palatable to cattle tend to be highly flammable and to hold the soil less well than native grasses. Overgrazing also re-duces the "organic litter" of brush and leaves that helps plants grow. When there is less plant cover, fewer roots re-main to hold soil together. The result is increased soil ero-sion from winds, rain, and floods. Overgrazing also contributes mightily to a decline in plant diversity, so es-sential to ecological health, putting more plants on the en-dangered list than any other cause. In *State of the World: 1995,* Lester Brown warned that:

> *Ecological burdens from intensive livestock operations in-clude loss of native vegetation, decline of fisheries as water is diverted for irrigation and stream habitats are degraded, dis-eases in native herbivores, and major changes in fire fre-quency, soils, hydrology, and other ecosystem processes. . . . Half of U.S. rangeland, most of it in the mountainous West, is now considered severely degraded, with its livestock carry-ing capacity reduced by at least 50 percent.*

At the same time, the manure of cattle is not, as one might expect, a countervailing factor that adds a rich supply of nu-trients to the land. In fact, the manure of range cattle returns to the land less than 25 percent of the nitrogen consumed by the cattle, in part because some of the nitrogen is lost in the formation of ammonia, a concomitant of cow manure. Worse, cow pies dry rapidly in the heat of the arid, over-grazed West, destroying the microorganisms that facilitate decomposition. As a result, the cow pies can remain intact for periods of years, often smothering the grass underneath.

That's twenty-five pounds' worth of dung per day per head of cattle helping to decorate the western landscape.

In a healthy ecological system, herbivores that are native to a region consume some of its plant life, absorbing nutrients from the plants and returning them to the soil as their own excretions decompose, and as the animals themselves, whose populations are controlled by natural forces, decompose after death. In the case of cattle, by contrast, we are dealing with outsized numbers (its population protected by human intervention) of a species not native to most regions in which it finds itself, consuming outsized quantities of plant life, then returning little of the nutrients to the soil because of the hardy nature of its manure and because the animals themselves generally do not die and decompose on the land, but are slaughtered in abattoirs, with most of what is not consumed by people recycled into pellets at rendering plants. Precious grams of nitrogen, phosphorus, and potassium escape the grassland ecosystems with each carcass of range-fed cattle.

In a healthy riparian environment, trees, bushes, grasses, and all manner of plant life surrounding streams provide dam-building material for diverse animal life, which in turn augments riparian health. Beaver, for instance, by making dams, are helpful in raising water tables, containing floods, and facilitating new riparian growth. Although beaver used to thrive in riparian environments throughout the land, they are now reduced to 2 percent of their original population. Plant life also provides a habitat for insects, which serve not only the soil but the water as well. Upon falling into the water with plant parts, insects become food for fish and other forms of aquatic life—up to 99 percent of aquatic nutrients come from adjacent plant life. When those plants are destroyed by grazing cattle, the food web that links land to water comes undone.

Plant life surrounding springs helps to shelter them as well, to build up the soil around them, and to raise water tables; when cattle trample and consume these plants, springs dry up. It has been estimated that tens of thousands of western springs have been wiped out by overgrazing.

Eighty to ninety percent of the riparian zones of such western states as Idaho, Colorado, Arizona, and New Mexico have been degraded almost out of existence by livestock grazing. Eighty-three percent of Wyoming's streams have been lost to grazing. Ranchers allow livestock to trample aquatic vegetation without the slightest regard for the role that vegetation plays in anchoring streambeds, filtering out sediments, and breaking down nutrients and pollutants.

The damage cattle have done to streams, riparian zones, and the once-lush grasslands of America has been rivaled by the devastation they have wreaked on our forests. As Lynn Jacobs explains: "Though few people realize it, Western forests are also heavily grazed, generally with higher livestock densities than on open landscapes. For a century, nearly every forest in the West, even in the soggy Northwest, has been degraded by livestock." Although the damage livestock inflict on forests is camouflaged by the fact that trees are left standing, the soil, stripped of grass and small plants, loses its capacity to retain moisture. The dangerous cycle of soil erosion is thus put into motion, leaving trees more likely to experience stunted growth or to be attacked by insects, and making it less likely that new trees will develop from seedlings struggling on dry, overgrazed ground. A test in the foothills of Northern California demonstrated that after five years of protection from livestock, a study plot had 554 oak saplings per acre. A plot of land grazed by sheep had zero saplings per acre.

It shouldn't be surprising that by damaging streams, grasslands, riparian zones, and forests, livestock wind up devastating other forms of animal life. Keep in mind that cattle are an invading species, not native to our continent. Whereas all animals native to the West evolved in harmony with their environment, finding their habitats and often their food in the plant life evolving around them, cattle were simply imposed on the land, and by voraciously consuming virtually all forms of plants, they act like heartless colonizers who run the natives off their territory and despoil all their resources. And they have an army on their side: the stockmen who hunt down and generally protect them from animals that would either kill them or compete with them for food, and who attend them with veterinary care and even, when necessary, extra feed. And of course government gets into the act, ceding its land to the stockmen, as there isn't big money in wildlife. The Bureau of Land Management, for example, grants livestock more than 90 percent of the allotted forage in its six resource areas in southern Idaho; all other wildlife combined are supposed to make do with less than 10 percent. If it were a case of survival of the fittest, cattle would not long thrive in the West. But it's not exactly a level playing field.

Cattle have displaced buffalo, elk, deer, pronghorn antelope, bighorn sheep, and moose, among other large herbivores that used to roam our continent in far greater numbers than they do today. These species currently struggle forth with only 1 to 3 percent of their primeval population. All these wild animals traditionally migrate as they forage, allowing regeneration of plant life, and never lazily foul and denude their environment the way domestic livestock do. The cattle culture's destructive impact on native species is felt in a myriad of ways. Pronghorn, deer, and other native ungulates, for example, like to hide their newborn in tall grass to protect them from predators. With cattle maintaining sovereignty over the land, tall grass is hard to find, and the newborn are left vulnerable. Grizzly bears experience nutritional deprivation from livestock grazing, and as a result suffer declining fertility. In sum, western ecosystems supported the behavior of those large grazing mammals that evolved within them; it is the intensive and widespread grazing of imposed livestock that these same ecosystems cannot sustain.

It's not only other land animals, but fish and birds that would plead with us, if only they could, to get rid of the livestock. A study of an Oregon wildlife refuge found bird counts five to seven times higher in its ungrazed areas, compared to similar areas grazed annually. A study of a river in Oregon found trout populations to be 350 percent higher in ungrazed portions than grazed areas. Due mostly to the degradation of riparian environments by livestock and the consequent pollution of our waterways, our native fishes are now the fastest-disappearing wildlife group in the United States.

You might think that America's wildlife is being protected by our system of National Wildlife Refuges. But of 109 such refuges in the states of Montana, Wyoming, Colorado, Utah, Kansas, Nebraska, and the Dakotas, 103 are grazed.

Just as European colonizers killed off more Native Americans by disease than by bullets, so our colonizing livestock have brought over diseases from the Old World that have decimated native animal populations in the New. Cattle and sheep spread disease and parasites to wildlife through infected water, manure, vegetation, and soil, flies and other insects, as well as through physical contact and the sharing of salt licks. Wild animals that eat dead cattle may also wind up wishing they had been more health-conscious and laid off beef.

The diseases livestock spread include anthrax, brucellosis, encephalitis, leptospirosis, pneumonia, bluetongue, pinkeye, scabies, and rabies. These diseases generally present some danger to humans as well as to wildlife. In addition, a seemingly limitless variety of worms, flies, and other parasitic organisms feast predominantly on cattle and sheep and then consider sampling other wildlife or humans for dessert.

The bovine is truly a formidable and resourceful killer in the disguise of an innocent, melancholy, big-eyed grass-eater. All kinds of animals have suffered under its domination of the West. Rabbits are endangered by the lack of vegetative cover for shelter and food; frogs, toads, and insects miss the rich, moist soil that livestock have dried and hardened; wild pigs are deprived of grasses, nuts, and berries; fish go belly-up in the cow-polluted streams and rivers; elk and antelope perish from diseases borne by livestock-spread bacteria; people get heart attacks, diabetes, and cancer.

In addition, animals as well as people are killed by devastating floods. Have you noticed that floods in this country seem to be getting worse, year by year? Is it just a streak of bad luck, or is something more at play? Let's consider the problem for a moment, and you may not be surprised if we need to round up the usual suspects.

Flooding constitutes perhaps the most dangerous and

most dramatic element of the pernicious cycle of soil erosion. In recent years, we have all witnessed horrendous news reports of flooding, particularly in the American West and Midwest. We have seen whole towns and cities immersed in water, homes adrift, people and pets rescued by helicopter or motorboat from the tops of cars or trees isolated by floodwaters. And we have been told that Nature has again taken its toll. The federal government usually attempts to help the affected citizenry recover, issuing check after check in the billions of dollars to the flood regions for relief. Most of us accept this cycle of punishment and recovery as acts of Nature beyond our control.

Well, to some extent, flooding is part of Nature's plan; certainly there will always be floods, and they will always take some toll. In fact, as an occasional occurrence, floods have many ecologically beneficial effects, such as freeing waterways from vegetation that may be choking them, spreading seeds, and building fertile bottomland. But with the advent of livestock grazing across the West, floods have gotten out of hand in both frequency and severity. In much of the West, serious flooding has historically mirrored the periods of the most prolific livestock grazing. The plants consumed by livestock tend to be those that are most efficient at conserving water. Water runoff from storms or melting snow that, in a healthy environment, would be retained by plants and percolated down into the soil and the aquifers below becomes a highly destructive force on dry, bare, overgrazed land.

Not only plants but also soil, and particularly topsoil, serve to retain water, acting as Nature's sponges. But more than half of western topsoil has been lost since livestock began overtaking the western plains 140 years ago. Topsoil is the most precious commodity a farmer has. It takes Nature anywhere between one hundred and eight hundred years to produce one inch of topsoil. Since the founding of the United States, Nature would have provided us with, at most, about two inches more of topsoil, but due to our chemical farming practices and our essential forfeiture of sovereignty over the land to cattle, we've lost about six inches. We are squandering a resource whose preciousness we don't even begin to understand, and floods are just part of our collective comeuppance.

Make no mistake: there are other factors that aggravate flooding. Logging, mining, road-building, and overdevelopment certainly play their part. But nothing compares in impact with the widespread crew-cutting of the earth by cattle. Nonetheless, the next time a flood ravages a city or a county in the Midwest or the West, you will not read the following in the newspaper the next day: "The devastation was wrought largely by our collective appetite for beef."

Well, don't disbelieve everything you don't read. The fact is, if we got the cattle off our land, and let the plant cover grow back, over time our problems with flooding would be greatly mitigated.

The dark, rich, loamy soil that came to my mind as I was awaiting my operation was created by millennia of vegetative cover and nourished by generations of organic farming practices. It was a precious commodity that I did not have the right to experiment with. Soil is a complex, delicate, mysterious thing. Maybe it is best thought of not as a thing so much as a process: an ongoing series of chemical reactions that, through a subtle interplay with living creatures, create an organic architecture that sustains life. Its importance cannot be overstated. Rachel Carson, in *Silent Spring*, wrote:

*The thin layer of soil that forms a patchy covering over the continents controls our own existence and that of every other animal of the land. Without soil, land plants as we know them could not grow, and without plants no animals could survive.*

*Yet if our agriculture-based life depends on the soil, it is equally true that soil depends on life, its very origins and the maintenance of its true nature being intimately related to living plants and animals.*

By introducing cattle in unnatural numbers onto marginal land where they do not belong in the first place, we are tampering dangerously with complex ecosystems. An insidious spiral develops: overgrazing leads to more dust and drier air (as less water transpires from vegetation), leading to less rain, resulting in still less plant life. Also, topsoil bared to the elements tends to experience greater extremes in temperature, destroying root systems and soil organisms. In the short run of a century or so, the damage to overgrazed land could result in the kind of desertification currently afflicting the American West, about 10 percent of which has reached the state at which it can barely support life. In the long run of several centuries, we in America could be creating another Sahara—for the Sahara itself was a region luxuriant with trees eight thousand years ago, before nomadic tribes began burning the trees to provide grazing for their herds.

Desertification is a global problem. More than one-third of the Earth's land surface has been desertified to some degree by livestock grazing. According to United Nations experts, deserts are expanding globally by 27,000 square miles

(70,000 square kilometers) annually, costing affected nations $42 billion a year. Africa and Asia, where more than half the population of the world lives, suffer the worst effects, but the threat is present in virtually all regions of the Earth. We might take a lesson from the Thar Desert, a wasteland roughly the size of Oregon in the Indus region of eastern Pakistan and northwestern India. Two thousand years ago it was densely vegetated. Today, after twenty centuries of livestock grazing, the land is barren, despite the fact that the air in the region is moist. Scientists speculate that the region's atmospheric dust hinders the formation of rain clouds.

Cattle injure even natural desert. Although its vegetation may appear sparse, natural desert nonetheless is alive with an appropriate mix of cacti, succulents, grasses, and shrubs. Cryptogamic crusts, which consist of layers of bacteria, algae, mosses, lichens, and microfungi, are a less visible form of plant cover found in arid regions. These crusts serve to hold water, moderate soil temperature, fix nitrogen, and actually create soil. You might consider them Nature's way of keeping deserts healthy and alive, and gradually turning deserts more verdant. These vulnerable crusts do not withstand trampling, and thus are destroyed by cattle. Their destruction plays a large role in the "cow-burning" of our deserts.

Even though it takes hundreds of acres of desert to sustain a cow for a year, western deserts are grazed more often than not. There are over a hundred ranchers grazing cattle on California's Mojave Desert alone. Such a bizarre use of land makes the work of the artist Christo, who has been known to wrap whole islands in pink fabric, look sensible and pragmatic by comparison. Here's how the absurd economics of the oxymoronic desert grazing works: permittees pay about a penny per acre per year, and to compensate even partially for the damage their cattle inflict, taxpayers have to kick in annually more money—for water pipelines, fencing, roads, and other capital improvements—than the cattle are worth.

There are few human accomplishments on the planet that are viewable from space. Two of them are the Great Wall of China, and the fires that are burning in the Brazilian rain forest. As many as seven thousand have been detected burning in the Amazon in one day, as ranchers find fire to be the quickest and most expedient way to clear land. More of Brazil is aflame now than ever before. An area about the size of Maine is cleared from the Amazon annually. While most Americans are concerned about rain forest destruction, few realize that cattle ranching stands as its salient cause. An estimated 70 percent of the clearing of the Amazon is for cattle pasture. In fact, "pasture" is perhaps too generous a term for what the cattle get. Rain forest topsoil is notoriously poor in nutrients and is fragile. Its mineral base is exhausted after a few short years of producing grass, and luxurious jungle degrades to desert in a wink of history.

Humanity is rich in folly, but it's hard to think of a folly more mind-bogglingly stupendous than that of transforming infinitely rich, diverse, dense jungle into desert in a few years' time for the sake of a few more hamburgers. This pernicious practice has historically been encouraged by the World Bank, which concerns itself foremost with the repayment of Brazil's international debt. It's been estimated that for every hamburger exported from Brazil in order to pay its debt, fifty-five square feet of rain forest must be cleared. Meanwhile, indigenous Amazonians, who know how to live in a sustainable fashion on forest products, are being displaced by rapacious ranchers, much as Native Americans were decimated by cattlemen on our continent. At the present rate of destruction, the Brazilian rain forest will cease to exist in fifty years' time. Like the cattle ranchers who despoil the American West, the ranchers of the Amazon produce marginal returns even for consumers of meat: only 3 to 4 percent of Brazilian beef is produced in the Amazon. Still, the destruction goes on, partly from greed and perceived economic imperative, partly from ignorance, and partly from the stubborn cultural attraction of the cowboy image. Catherine Caufield explains the latter phenomenon this way:

> . . . *In San José and Brasília, and throughout the Latin tropics, dentists and lawyers establish their manliness and their connection to the aristocratic Spanish past by becoming cattlemen. Cattle ranching makes no sense for large parts of the continent; nonetheless great areas of land are being degraded, and millions of peasants are short of food because of the Iberians' overwhelming atavistic urge to become a caballero.*

As a former caballero myself, I can only tell you that I don't see what all the fuss is about. The job sure as hell didn't seem real glamorous to me.

Ultimately, the oxygen lost due to rain forest destruction will be lost to the entire world, as will the biodiversity that could provide scientific and pharmaceutical breakthroughs. Thus, while national sovereignty must be respected in finding a solution to the senseless destruction, national borders remain morally irrelevant to the crisis. The world has an obligation and an interest in helping induce Brazil to save its own forest.

Mexico's largest rain forest, the semitropical Selva Lacandona, while considerably smaller than the Amazon, boasts more native mammalian species than the Brazilian forest. Its Barbasco vine provided the ingredients of the first birth control pill. The forest supports half the animal and plant species of Mexico. The Lacandona is being threatened by a combination of population pressures, political policies, and destructive farming techniques, notably cattle grazing. In the 1970s, the government of Mexico, unwilling to redistribute vast estates controlled by wealthy land barons, encouraged landless peasants to settle in the Lacandona. Today three hundred thousand people inhabit forest villages, and they have destroyed almost half of the four-million-acre forest.

Typically the Lacandonan forest villagers use slash-and-burn techniques to clear sections of ancient forest, then plant corn or other crops on the land for a year or two, until the thin forest topsoil is depleted. At that point, they allow cattle to graze the abandoned pastures. After three to five years, the cattle leave bare bedrock in their wake.

More than half of Mexico is grazed by livestock. Most wildlife—wolves, bears, jaguars, mountain lions—have been removed from the Mexican landscape. More of Mexico's grain is fed to cattle than to people.

The plague of cattle that threatens Mexico and the Amazon has devastated much of the rest of South and Central America. One hundred fifty million cattle and eighty million sheep overgraze southern Brazil, Argentina, and Uruguay. Half of Colombia, Venezuela, and Bolivia is dedicated to grazing as well, as is half of Central America and two-thirds of its arable land. As Catherine Caufield writes, "One reason that the Central American rainforests seem doomed to disappear is that their destruction takes five cents off the price of an American hamburger."

A century ago, Central American land was blanketed with forest and blessed with some of the greatest diversity of plant and animal species on Earth. Today it produces steaks for those in Central America who can afford them, and exports hamburger to the United States. As much as 90 percent of Latin American beef exports end up in North America, often in the form of fast-food hamburgers.

The devastation is not only ecological, but economic as well. Rain forest cattle ranches tend to employ about one person per twelve square miles. Subsistence farming, by contrast, can support as many as a hundred people per square mile. Chris C. Park notes in his book *Tropical Rainforests* that when primeval forest is given over to ranchers, "The developing country makes no money from the transaction other than the price the land was originally sold for; all profits from ranching are enjoyed by the owners of the ranches." The forest of infinite riches is inevitably sold at a cheap price. At the same time, the inequalities of land ownership in Central American nations and the export-driven patterns of agriculture there have left large segments of their populations marginalized, while the beef produced on their land is consumed by people in the United States, and by our pets.

It's humbling to think that, even after turning over the greater share of our public land to cattle ranchers, and in spite of the massive feedlot operations fouling our country, we Americans still need to *import* beef to satisfy our collective demand for heart attacks. In the process, we facilitate the chopping down of Central and South American rain forest, while leaving the populations of those countries impoverished.

Similar ecological degradation has occurred all over the world, including the Caribbean islands, where Columbus in 1493 lamentably introduced cattle, sheep, pigs, goats, and horses. As much as half of some of these islands' original forest has been converted to cattle pasture. On the other side of the globe, two-thirds of Australia is given up to grazing its one hundred and sixty million sheep and thirty million cattle. Ranchers walk hand in glove with timbermen to decimate the once-ubiquitous rain forests of the Philippines. The timbermen come in first, take the wood, then leave pasture for the cattlemen, who prevent reforestation. Even Japan, with so little land and such intense population pressures, somehow finds the room for pasture for several million cattle. Northern and western China are threatened by desertification brought about by sheep and goat production. Livestock have endangered as well the delicate ecosystems of the Himalaya and Mongolia. Eastern Europe and the former states of the Soviet Union have had the Earth's greatest increase in the population of cattle in the last fifty years. India, home of the "sacred cow"—or rather two hundred million of them—along with fifty million sheep, has lost forest at an alarming rate. It has the dubious distinction of being probably the most overgrazed country in the world. The ecological consequences will be unthinkably severe for a population verging on one billion, many of whom burn the dung of livestock for fuel, further depriving the soil.

Around the globe, wherever the onslaught of ranching is felt, forest is lost, native flora and fauna face extinction, streams and rivers are polluted, soil erosion worsens, topsoil blows off in the wind or runs off overgrazed hills, dust storms arise, and Nature plots her revenge in the form of desert.

And with desert will come famine.

# CHAPTER EIGHT

# Skip the Miracles and Eat Well

Now I bet I know what some of you are thinking. *Helping to save the Earth with a vegetarian diet would be great, but what's it going to do for my figure?*

Here's the good news: if you're looking to slim down, you almost undoubtedly will. If you already feel fit, a vegetarian diet will keep you that way. On the average, vegetarians in America weigh about twenty pounds less than meat-eaters. If you compare the populations of nations like China and India, where the diet is largely plant-based and obesity is comparatively rare, to the populations of heavy meat-eating countries like Germany, Canada, and the United States, where obesity is common, you get your first clue about what meat does to your weight.

America is the most overweight country in the world. Over 70 percent of all Americans are overweight. One-third of all Americans are obese (defining obesity as at least 20 percent overweight). Children, especially little girls, often begin dieting in the early years of grade school, and the obsession with weight may follow them all their lives. Every year or two there's a new diet craze that sweeps the country, racking up millions of dollars in profits for whoever writes the book, and yet not making a noticeable dent in the obesity statistics. It's a good racket. Should you want to get into it, just come up with a catchy title—say, *The Cake and Shake Miracle Diet*—tell a personal story about how you wondrously lost twelve pounds the week you discovered the synergistic dietetic properties of cheesecake washed down with a chocolate malted, improvise a little bit (preferably with complex-sounding scientific snippets of information that leave the reader perplexed but in awe of your learning) about why other diets don't work and yours does, commiserate with dieters about how they've been led astray by all those ineffective and painfully difficult diets, include a whole bunch of recipes, and those millions can be yours.

Some of these dieting fads have been known to do worse than merely take people's money without producing the promised results. The most tragic recent case is that of the once-popular diet drug combination of fenfluramine and phentermine ("fen-phen"), which has caused valvular heart disease in otherwise healthy people. The FDA, guilty of having allowed the drugs to linger on the market until more than ninety people developed heart valve disease, now estimates that as many as 30 percent of those who got suckered into taking the drugs may wind up with serious heart valve damage.

Americans turn to dieting fashions out of frustration with conflicting nutritional information. Nutrition has become, like economics, a science so rife with theory and argumentation that the public comes to the conclusion that there are no laws, that no expert truly knows anything, and that one guess is as good as another.

Well, in fact, that's only true of economics.

I'm a believer in simplicity. When a theory about something as basic as diet starts getting too complicated for a normal person to grasp, I start getting awfully suspicious. And that's only the first reason why I'm awfully suspicious of one of the latest dieting fads, the dangerous nonsense marketed as the "Zone" diet by Dr. Barry Sears. Sears has sold six million copies of his diet books, and I–as well as many nutritionists–worry for the health of anyone who takes him seriously. At the risk of giving his diet more attention than it's worth, let's take a good look at how a fad diet like the Zone manages to oversimplify the facts and misinform the reader in a way that just happens to help sell books.

Sears begins from a premise that works well for selling diet books: *Tell 'em what they want to hear.* He recommends eating a diet in which 30 percent of calories come from fat–far higher than the percentages recommended by the Pritikin diet, or by such prominent nutritionists as Dean Ornish and John McDougall, but identical to the recommendation of the more conservative (some might say, meat- and dairy-industry-influenced) National Academy of Sciences, and nearly equal to–in fact, a tad lower than–the actual current percentage of fat in the typical American diet. So Sears's fat intake recommendation is hardly bitter medicine for a fat country accustomed to eating fatty foods. In Sears's own words, his diet "doesn't rob food of most of its flavor, as do many of the extremely low-fat diets. In fact, I can even show you how to stay within these dietary guidelines while eating at fast-food restaurants. And yes, you can still have your Häagen-Dazs." Ah, now *there's* a diet.

Sears makes the case for his diet by contending that over

the last ten years, Americans have been hammered over the head with low-fat, high-carbohydrate diets espoused by such nutrition experts as Pritikin, Ornish, and McDougall, and yet have grown only fatter. Therefore, he claims that the low-fat, high-carbo mantra is wrongheaded, and that a better way to lose weight would be to eat more fat, as part of his recommended 40-30-30 Zone diet, in which 40 percent of calories come from carbohydrates, and 30 percent each from fat and protein. In other words, *pass the ice cream, please, I feel like dieting.*

Why have Americans grown fatter in spite of the low-fat recommendations of established nutritionists? Here's the stunning answer, and it's hard to believe Sears doesn't know it. *Most Americans have not been on Pritikin, Ornish, or McDougall diets!* In fact, over the last decade, the percentage of fat in the standard American diet has come down only slightly–from about a whopping 37 to 38 percent of calories in 1980 to an almost as dangerous 33 to 34 percent today. Why has the percentage of fat in the American diet come down even that much? Not because absolute intake of fat has declined at all, but only because the average American has increased his caloric intake, usually in the form of empty carbohydrates–in other words, refined sugars. It's like adding sugar to your cheeseburger, and saying, "Hey, the percentage of fat in my diet has just come down, how come I'm not losing weight?"

Those comparatively few people who have followed the Pritikin, Ornish, or McDougall programs, by contrast, have tended to do quite well. Ornish has had such success in reversing heart disease (as well as helping people lose weight) that in September 1997, Medicare announced a policy of reimbursing patients for the cost of attending his clinic. Häagen-Dazs, alas, is not recommended eating on his diet.

Although Sears is pretty much telling Americans to keep eating the way they already eat (although, as we shall see, in smaller quantities, and with a calculator), his prescription sounds high-tech, complex, and mathematically precise.

> . . . *You must eat food in a controlled fashion and in the proper proportions—as if it were an intravenous drip. Reaching the Zone is a matter of technology. . . .*
> . . . *The dietary technology required to reach the Zone is as precise as any computer technology.*

It's of course reassuring to note that this advanced technology is obtainable at fast-food joints. The right balance of hot dogs, hamburgers, milk shakes, and fries will apparently keep you "in the Zone" of optimal health. But while you're at the fast-food joints, Sears wants you to be thinking about your *glycemic index*—that's the entry rate of carbohydrates into the bloodstream. Certain foods have a higher glycemic index than others, and are best avoided. Among these shunned foods are puffed-rice cakes. Luckily, Sears is quick to point out that ice cream has a fitness-producing low-glycemic index.

> . . . *too many high-glycemic carbohydrates can not only make you fat, they will also keep you that way. . . . Virtually all fruits (except bananas and dried fruits) and virtually all fiber-rich vegetables (except carrots and corn) are low-glycemic carbohydrates. Virtually all grains, starches, and pasta are high-glycemic carbohydrates.*

As usual, Sears tries to make reality conform with his diet. As nutritionist Jennifer Raymond points out, the glycemic index of foods is considered unreliable by the American Diabetes Association. It "varies depending on whether you eat the food cooked or raw; whether you eat it alone, or with other foods; whether it's canned or prepared at home; whether you grew it or bought it at the grocery store; whether you add salt, or don't add salt—all of these factors affect the glycemic index. . . . And yet Barry Sears builds his case on this."

I would agree with Sears that not all carbohydrates are equal, and that fruits and vegetables are to be preferred over such products as bagels and pasta made from refined white flour. Beyond that, I think he overstates his case—if he has any case at all—in asking us to worry about dietary factors that are imperfectly understood and may be more or less irrelevant to our health. When I eat, I like to enjoy myself, not worry about whether I'm going to "hit the correct key strokes" while treating my food "as if it were an intravenous drip." That's just a little bit too contrived for this farm boy.

As if watching your glycemic index weren't difficult enough, Sears recommends getting an appropriate balance of insulin and eicosanoids—hormones that help regulate the immune system. According to Sears, "high levels of insulin generated by too much carbohydrate drive you out of the Zone by decreasing the production of good eicosanoids and increasing the production of bad ones." It's just that simple.

Sears also has an original take on fiber, contradicting the nutritional establishment, which has come to appreciate its many beneficial effects on human health. Although he seems to approve of fiber when it encases carbohydrates, he seems to be *against* it when it encases protein:

*Vegetable protein tends to be encased in a high-fiber network. Animal sources of protein have no fiber, and thus have a higher degree of digestibility. So vegetable sources of protein will not give the same gram-for-gram absorption of amino acids as animal-protein sources.*

I haven't seen any evidence for these assertions. I've yet to see the study that proves that plant-derived protein is in any way inferior to animal-derived protein. (Advocates of the homocysteine hypothesis of heart disease, as we shall see, in fact make the opposite case: that plant-derived protein is superior to animal protein.) But I have seen countless studies of the benefits of fiber. We know that a fiber-deficient diet can result in deadly colon cancer—the leading cause of cancer-related death in nonsmokers—and we've seen how nations with heavy meat, fiber-deficient diets have demonstrably greater incidence of colon cancer. Sears is, as far as I know, the only scientist in America to make a case of any kind against fiber. In making such insupportable assertions, I believe he's playing a dangerous game with people's health.

As if to disassociate his own diet from failed diets of its type, Sears attacks high-protein regimes for inducing the abnormal metabolic state known as ketosis, in which abnormal biochemicals called ketone bodies are manufactured by stressed cells and excreted through increased urination. The result of such diets is usually, he notes accurately, a temporary loss of weight—water weight. As Sears points out, "more than 95% of the people who have ever lost weight using high-protein ketogenic diets have gained that weight back and more."

What he doesn't point out is that many people who lose

weight at first on his own diet may be going down precisely that road. Remember, the human body cannot store excess protein. We literally piss away all that we can't use. And the Zone diet pegs our need for protein, as a percentage of dietary intake, at a high level—far too high, in my opinion. Those who, despite the almost hidden caloric restriction that (as we shall see) is implicit in the Zone diet, retain normal caloric dietary levels while taking in 30 percent of their calories as protein, risk the long-term weight gain, kidney stress, and other health problems (including osteoporosis) associated with a ketogenic diet.

The Zone diet takes it cue from other diets proportionally high in protein and fat, like the Atkins and Scarsdale diets. Since carbohydrates hold more water than protein, these ketogenic diets often get dieters off to a fast and enthusiastic start in losing water weight—and then dieters tend to hit resistance unless they severely limit their caloric intake. These diets appeal to people who don't have the nerve to attempt real change in their fatty, animal-based diets, as well as to those who have failed at "low-fat" diets—usually from some combination of eating too many empty, allegedly "low-fat" junk-food calories, being fooled into believing that certain dairy products were actually "low-fat" as labeled, believing wrongly that fish, chicken, or "lean" cuts of meat were low-fat, and not exercising.

None of these high-animal-protein diets' advocates, of course, make a point of warning people of the risks of colon cancer, osteoporosis, or heart disease that come with the bargain. Sears all but dismisses the role of dietary cholesterol as a factor in heart disease, a role so well established that he might as well be arguing that the Earth is flat.

Let's say you decide, out of desperation, to try the Zone

diet. You decide to treat food like a powerful drug or an intravenous drip, making sure you're getting the scientifically proven, correct 40-30-30 balance of macronutrients, eating the appropriate number of "carbohydrate blocks," "protein blocks," and "fat blocks." You wake up in the morning full of resolve to embark on this new, meticulously engineered diet. You determine your unique protein needs, following Sears's instructions to factor in your percentage of body fat and your precise level of physical activity. Once you have established your unique protein requirement, you can deduce your unique fat and carbohydrate requirements. Next, you pour out your bowl of corn flakes for breakfast, and you check the box to see how many grams of fat, protein, and carbohydrate are in each serving. Since your corn flakes are unfortunately (by Sears's standards) high in carbohydrates and low in fat and protein, you decide to add some extra-fatty buttermilk to restore the meal to the ideal Zone balance. You perform some calculations, and determine that you'll need to add, say, two and three-quarters glasses of buttermilk to your cereal to reach the magical 40-30-30 Zone. You consider adding a handful of raisins but by now you lack the mental energy for the math and all the calculations have left you late for work. The cereal tastes kind of soggy, but you don't care because you're in the Zone, the almost metaphysical region where you know that "the mind is relaxed, yet alert and exquisitely focused. Meanwhile, the body is fluid, strong, and apparently indefatigable. It's almost euphoric. There are no distractions, and time seems to slow down to a graceful waltz." Surely all that is worth the price of soggy, fatty cereal. In order to stay in this ethereal region, you determine to psychically monitor (you don't know how else it could be done) your insulin levels throughout the rest of the day, while keeping a third eye on obtaining your optimal balance of "good" and "bad" eicosanoids. Meanwhile you've got your finger on the pulse of the glycemic index of all the foods you consider putting into your system. For lunch, you decide to buy a chicken salad sandwich. Although no one in the deli can answer your questions about the sandwich's macronutrient content, you look at it real closely and it definitely looks like a 40-30-30 sandwich. Anyway, it tastes Zone-friendly, and you resolve to adhere to the diet more strictly at dinner. You're doing reasonably well so far, but when you start thinking about what to cook for dinner, suddenly staying in the Zone seems daunting. It was hard enough to take a bowl of cereal for breakfast and a sandwich for lunch, but how do you stay within the magical 40-30-30 Zone of optimal health when you want to cook a meal with a lot of different ingredients? You begin to wonder, where is all this science leading me?

To *turkey escalopes fontina*. Yes, that's what Sears recommends in his chapter "Your Dietary Road Map to the Zone." Apparently, twelve ounces of thin-sliced turkey breast, a half teaspoon of olive oil, a teaspoon of butter, some salt and pepper, two cloves of garlic, no less than fifteen sprigs of parsley, one half cup of chicken stock, and one ounce of shredded Fontina cheese, correctly prepared, will lead you to the technologically precise Zone in which your eicosanoids will be in heaven. New England Bouillabaisse, Lamb with Garlic Cheese and Vegetable Pasta, and Poached Haddock with Hot Green Beans and Artichokes will get you there as well, at least if you follow the scientifically developed, high-tech, state-of-the-art recipes in Sears's book.

There's a glaring contradiction between Sears's admonition to follow his magical formula of 40-30-30 in macronutrient intake—a formula to be followed during each meal and each snack, no less—and his inclusion of meat sources as an acceptable, indeed even a preferable, source of protein. The contradiction derives from the near-impossibility of knowing how much fat is truly in each serving of meat. And saturated fat, which even Sears isn't high on, and which we know contributes to heart attacks and strokes, makes up the greater share of animal fat.

If only Sears took his own advice, he might at least be able to boast that measure of integrity. But I doubt that he does. According to Sears, the protein requirement is unique for each individual; based on that protein requirement, a person's optimal intake of fat and carbohydrates can be calculated. Factoring in his weight, percentage of body fat, and level of physical activity, he found his own protein requirement to be 100 grams daily, or 400 calories from protein. That means he should get another 400 calories from fat and 533 calories from carbohydrates. His total daily caloric intake: 1,333 calories. This is prima facie evidence of the absurdity of his diet. Sears is six foot five and over two hundred pounds. Any reputable nutritionist would recommend that a man his size take in at least 2,000, and perhaps as much as 2,700 calories per day. On 1,333 calories, he would be virtually starving himself and risking nutritional deficiencies. He would certainly lose weight, but only because of a severe shortage in caloric intake. Sears writes, "Calories don't count, but protein does," and yet his diet is absurdly low-calorie. Starvation diets will always make you lose weight at first, but ultimately they are counterproductive both to human health and to long-term weight loss. And so the hidden truth about the Zone diet is that it is not actually what it is often thought to be: a high-protein, high-fat diet. It is instead—for those who manage to follow it accurately—an extremely low-calorie, low-carbohydrate diet. But the complexity of Sears's presentation obscures the fact that, correctly followed, the diet would leave you very hungry. Interestingly, at one point in his book *Enter the Zone,* he virtually acknowledges as much:

> . . . *But what about total calories? After all, many diets are based on nothing more than cutting down your calorie consumption.*
>
> *In the Zone, your calorie needs don't change, but where they come from does. If you can meet a large portion of your calorie needs by more effectively accessing your internal stored body fat, then* you don't have to put as many external calories into your mouth. *[emphasis mine]*

Back where I come from, the word for putting "external calories into your mouth" is *eating.* Sears is saying, in his own recondite way, that you won't be eating as much as normal on his diet. While he manages to be very clear when he promises you that you'll be able to eat Häagen-Dazs and go to fast-food joints on his diet, he resorts to euphemisms when he informs you exactly how much, or how little, you'll be eating. In saying your *calorie needs* won't change on his diet, he utters mere gibberish. Of course your *calorie needs* won't change; what will apparently change is your ability to meet them on his diet.

There is a reason why low-calorie, starvation diets like the Zone ultimately fail: the human body does not know that it's on a diet. If the body doesn't get its caloric needs met, it assumes it's starving, and adopts the sensible strategy of storing more fat and lowering its rate of metabolism. We have all heard overweight people complain that they don't eat much, that they simply have slow metabolism. In fact, they're often right, and it's frequently the case that they have unwittingly slowed down their metabolism over the years by engaging in a counterproductive cycle of dieting (restricting caloric intake) and bingeing. Skinny people often take in more calories per day than fat people; usually the reason that they remain slim is that they have fast metabolic rates. Metabolism is the process by which food is converted into living tissue and energy to carry out the body's functions. A fast metabolism may be a genetic favor or may be induced by greater physical exercise or by a diet high in carbohydrates and low in fat. Ideally, what you want to do when trying to lose weight is to gently speed up your rate of metabolism. Your weight loss will be gradual but lasting, in contrast to the familiar yo-yo cycle of losing weight quickly by restricting calories and then gaining it back (and then some) by bingeing when the starvation diet inevitably ends. It is an ironic fact of life that dieting in the long run can make you fat.

A sound way to understand weight loss has been proposed by Dr. Terry Shintani, who runs a clinic in Hawaii. Dr. Shintani developed an index, the EMI (Eat More Index), that shows how many pounds of any given food would provide a full day's intake of 2,500 calories. Keep in mind that the average person needs to eat three to four pounds of food a day to satisfy hunger. The EMI for Cheddar cheese, for example, is 1.4, meaning that by eating nothing else all day but 1.4 pounds of Cheddar cheese, you would have consumed a full day's calories. The EMI for ham is 2.1, for fried chicken 2.2. Compare those figures to vegetarian foods. For brown rice, 4.6; potatoes, 9.5; carrots, 13.0; green beans,

21.8; eggplant, 28.7. In other words, if you fill your caloric needs with a pure eggplant diet, you're going to have to eat 28.7 pounds of it a day. I don't recommend it, but you sure as hell wouldn't be left hungry!

I don't claim to be a fitness expert, but I can offer the lesson of my own experience. Since I became a vegetarian eight years ago, I have lost 130 pounds steadily, gradually, and without trying. I never gained any of the weight back, and never felt hungry. I never went on a diet, never counted my calories, weighed my food, worried about my eicosanoids, consulted a chart of glycemic indexes, took any pills, or deprived myself one iota. I simply stopped eating animal products. I'm still losing a pound or two a month. As I lost the weight, my cholesterol count declined from over 300 to 140, my blood pressure went from dangerously high levels to normal ones, and my energy levels increased.

While there may be many competing approaches to weight loss, there is a consensus among most reputable nutritionists about three basic rules. To lose weight effectively and lastingly, the first rule is to *not* restrict your caloric intake, unless you are truly a compulsive overeater (and most overweight people are not) who eats far too many calories daily. Eat until you are satisfied. Generally, an average-sized woman should consume about 2,000 calories a day; an average-sized man about 2,500–but it varies widely with activity and metabolic levels. For most people eating normal-sized portions, there's little need to bother with calorie counting, and it's hard to do accurately anyway. Remember that people in China tend to eat more calories than Americans and yet stay slimmer because they consume a plant-based diet. But saying that you don't need to count calories is not the same thing as saying that calories don't count. If you eat enormous quantities of low-fat junk food packed with sugar, those calories will come back to haunt you.

The second rule is to eat a low percentage of your calories in the form of fat. In spite of what Barry Sears writes, *fat does make you fat*. There are nine calories in a gram of fat, whereas there are only four in a gram of carbohydrate. In addition, as Dr. Neal Barnard writes in his simple and authoritative *A Physician's Slimming Guide,* "Calories from carbohydrates are not as likely to increase body fat as the same number of calories from fats." This is because fat can be added directly to fat storage areas on our bodies. In order for carbohydrates to be stored, they have to first be converted to fat, a process that itself consumes calories. Furthermore, carbohydrates boost metabolism, allowing calories to be burned off at a faster clip. The high percentage of fat in the American diet stands unrivaled as the leading cause of obesity in this country. Although the ideal percentage of fat in the diet remains open to dispute, it's safe to say that for most people the optimal range falls somewhere between 10 and 15 percent of calories as fat. (Growing children and pregnant women may well have a need for a higher percentage of fat in their diets.) If you're concerned with dietary fat content as it relates to weight loss, you have to find out what works best for you. Keep in mind, though, that if you're eating the right kinds of foods, you won't need to know the exact percentage of fat in your diet; you'll naturally be in an appropriate range. Do not be fooled by the label *low-fat* on milk; such labels are misleading because they report the fat content as a percentage of weight rather than as a percentage of calories. Most of the weight of milk is water. *Milk labeled 2 percent fat is actually 35 percent fat as a percentage of calories,* and as such remains a high-fat food. The only useful statistics regarding fat are those that give the percentage of calories provided as fat, or that give the grams of fat in a serving. To give the fat content as a percentage of weight is highly misleading and ought to be banned as deceptive advertising.

The best way to avoid a high-fat diet is to abstain from all animal products. "Extra-lean" ground beef provides about 54 percent of its calories in the form of fat. Fifty-one percent of the calories of a roasted chicken come from fat, as do 40 percent of the calories of salmon. By contrast, less than 1 percent of the calories of a potato come from fat. As long as you don't consume the potato in the form of french fries (which can increase its fat content by more than two hundred times!), or top the potato with cheese, butter, or sour cream, it's an excellent low-fat food. Steamed or baked, topped with ketchup (look for organic brands, made without white sugar) or salsa or parsley or low-fat mushroom sauce or eaten plain, potatoes are a fine choice if you're watching your waistline. In place of animal foods, choose any complex carbohydrates—fruits, vegetables, grains, or beans—and they will help make you or keep you slim. Salads are good choices, as long as you don't pour high-fat dressing on them. Try using lemon juice, or some other fat-free dressing.

Eating a low-fat diet also means avoiding or limiting your intake of vegetable oils, margarine, nuts, seeds, olives, and avocados. Even a vegan diet may not help you lose weight, or lower your blood cholesterol levels, if you replace meats with large helpings of guacamole, peanut butter, fried vegetables, white bread smothered in margarine, pasta soaked in olive oil, doughnuts, and potato chips. It is unusual but certainly possible to gain weight on a vegan diet, and oils (which are

100 percent fat) and nuts (which are all extremely high fat) tend to be the prime culprits when this occurs. To the extent that you do use oil, canola oil is the best choice because it has the lowest percentage (6 percent) of saturated fat–but, remember, it's still 100 percent fat. Even if you are not seeking to lose weight, you should use these fatty foods only in moderation. Margarine, which contains hydrogenized oil, is not the healthy alternative many people believe it to be. As a risk to your heart and your health, it rivals the butter it seeks to replace.

Eating "low-fat" cookies, ice cream, or other snack foods won't help you lose weight. These foods tend to contain plenty of calories, and no fiber. Sometimes the fat content isn't really as low as the deceptive packaging suggests. Most important, these are empty calories, and you want your caloric intake to be working for you, providing your cells with nutrition.

The third fundamental rule of weight loss is, of course, to exercise. Exercising frequently in moderation has been shown to have health advantages when compared to infrequent, but longer and more vigorous, workouts. You are advised to consult a physician before starting an exercise program. You might want to consult as well the volume *Make the Connection,* by Bob Greene and Oprah Winfrey, in which Greene's exercise and weight-loss tips are accompanied by Oprah's personal diaries, written as she successfully undertook Greene's program. Everything Greene writes seems to me eminently sensible, with the single exception that I believe he should be emphasizing not just a low-fat diet but a low-fat *vegetarian* diet. Remember that seemingly "lean" cuts of beef will have saturated fat marbled throughout. And no matter how "lean" meat may seem, it provides unwanted cholesterol, which exists in the muscle.

All your food should come from what Dr. Neal Barnard calls the "The New Four Food Groups": fruit, vegetables, whole grains, and legumes (beans, peas, and lentils). There is an endless variety of meals to be created from these ingredients. Here's what I recommend. Take a stroll down the aisles of your favorite local natural foods store. Look at products you've never looked at before. Whenever possible, choose products that are organic, or that contain at least some organically produced ingredients. Remember, organic foods are going to have far higher levels of vitamins, minerals, and enzymes than foods grown chemically. When buying bread, look for organic whole grain bread. Avoid the empty calories of white bread. Buy organic brown rice, if available, rather than refined white rice. Similarly, organic whole wheat couscous is better for you than refined couscous. In place of the sort of sugar-laden, refined cereal products of which you can find a panoply in your commercial grocery, choose an organic whole grain cereal.

How can you have cold cereal, you wonder, on a vegan diet? Simple. Instead of cow's milk, explore a whole new world of nutritious, low-fat milks that contain not a trace of bovine growth hormone: rice milk, almond milk, oat milk, and soy milk. They come in all kinds of varieties with all kinds of flavorings, and they are delicious. Be adventurous. Let your taste buds adapt to new tastes and textures. If you've never tried the soy products tofu and tempeh, buy some and try preparing them in different ways. There are all manner of vegetarian cookbooks with countless recipes to help you. You may find several brands of seitan, a "wheat meat" made from gluten, to sample. You'll find tofu-based "hot dogs" that taste so much like the real thing—especially when topped with mustard, onions, and sauerkraut—that the only way you'll know they're vegetarian is that they won't give you a heart attack. You'll likely find all kinds of grain "burgers" and other meat analogues—fake bacon, ham, bologna, and turkey—usually made from soy protein and wheat gluten. They tend to be very low in fat and high in protein. You may like some and not like others, but they're all worth giving a try. There is even a variety of vegan "ice cream" products, usually made from rice or soy derivatives, and concentrated fruit sugars. Some, but not all of them, are low- or even zero-fat.

You may like some of these new foods immediately; some you may never like; some may grow on you over time. As a general rule, make sure that the level of fat in the products you choose is low, remembering that ingredients are listed on boxes in decreasing order of quantity. Choose products with a minimum of oil and sugar, and without artificial additives. Most important, make fresh fruits, fresh vegetables, legumes, and grains the heart of your diet. Make sure you're getting plenty of fiber—six or more servings a day of fresh fruits and vegetables—and keep the refined products to a minimum.

If you don't live within reasonable distance of a health food store, you may have difficulty obtaining some of the meat analogues and vegetarian specialty foods, but you still should have no trouble constructing a diet of fruits, vegetables, legumes, and grains. You could also look into the possibility of mail-ordering the vegetarian specialty foods from a catalog.

Farmers' markets are popping up all over the country. They are an ideal way to get fresh, healthy produce to consumers, with minimal expenditures of energy. With the middleman and packagers cut out of the action, the cost of farm-fresh goods is usually very reasonable. If there's a farmers' market in your area, by all means shop there. Seek out produce grown organically, and support your local farmers. Organically grown food sometimes costs a bit more than chemically grown food, but remember that by buying organic, you're getting greater nutritional value for your buck, you're avoiding pesticide residues, and you're helping farmers restore the Earth. You're also helping to preserve the tradition of family farming, since most organic farms are small-scale operations.

You'll find that the volume of food you eat on a vegetarian diet will often be greater than it was on a meat-based diet. Fibrous vegetarian food is naturally lower in calories and higher in nutrients than animal-based food. So you may find yourself eating more and losing weight, if you need to, at the same time. You will probably find—if you care to measure such things—that, in contrast to the Zone diet, about 10 to 15 percent of your calories will come from protein, about 10 to 15 percent from fat, and about 70 to 80 percent from carbohydrates. But if you shop for sensible vegan foods and eat plenty of fresh fruits and vegetables, you won't have to take out your calculator to see if you're hitting these goals—your intake will fall naturally into this healthy range.

You may need to adjust your methods of cooking as well. Make a practice of steaming, not frying, your vegetables. When you do choose to fry your food, try using water instead of oil. You'll be surprised at how well it works. Sautéing in wine, soy sauce, vinegar, or tomato juice is also an option that is preferable to oil.

Let's say that you've always eaten the traditional American diet. You might on an average day have bacon and eggs for breakfast; a cheeseburger for lunch; a steak with well-buttered potatoes for dinner, and ice cream for dessert. (That's basically how I used to eat on the farm, but in spades: a half dozen scrambled eggs with six slices of bacon for breakfast; a half-pounder for lunch, pork and beans on the side; a 16-ounce rib-eye steak for dinner, with mashed potatoes smothered in gravy made from steak drippings—the whole meal topped off with at least a pint of ice cream drowned in chocolate syrup!)

Now you've read this book, and you're ready to make a change. But you don't think you can make the "extreme" commitment of becoming a vegetarian, much less a vegan. Couldn't you maybe, you wonder, just have your eggs without bacon for breakfast, have your hamburger without cheese for lunch, cut down the steaks to maybe twice a week, have your potatoes with margarine, eat more fish and chicken, and try a vegetarian dinner once a week or so? Wouldn't that be good enough, at least for a start?

It's not what I'd recommend. Remember, fish and chicken are neither plant foods nor health foods. They present almost the exact same health risks as red meat: they are high in cholesterol (almost as high as red meat), high in fat, and possess no fiber. Eggs will provide you with enormous quantities of cholesterol even without the side of bacon. Margarine is scarcely more healthful than butter. If you feel you can only make such small, incremental changes in your diet, I don't want to discourage you from getting started, but neither do I want to encourage you to believe that you'll be doing yourself a lot of good—or even any good at all. You will still be damaging your arteries, even if the rate of damage decelerates minimally. The best analogy is to cigarette smoking. Is it a good idea to cut down from a two-pack-a-day habit to one pack a day? It's probably better than nothing, but it hardly eliminates the risk of lung cancer. Some former smokers say it's easier to quit cold turkey; others favor the gradual approach. In the case of diet, where physical addiction doesn't come into play, change shouldn't be as difficult.

I remember that when I decided to become a vegetarian, I assumed that by merely abstaining from flesh I was doing all that was necessary to restore my health. And so I became the world's worst vegetarian. For breakfast I'd have a glass of orange juice, an omelette with mushrooms and peppers, four to six slices of toast liberally smeared with butter and jelly, coffee, and a sweet roll. For lunch, I'd have a grilled cheese sandwich, with a two-pint can of beans and potato salad, followed by a slice of cherry pie and ice cream. This would tide me over till a mid-afternoon snack of doughnuts, an apple, and a diet soda. For supper, I might take a large lettuce salad, a liberal serving of pasta in marinara sauce smothered with Parmesan cheese, ending with at least a pint of low-fat ice cream with sprinkles. Before going to sleep, a handful of cookies kept me from feeling deprived– and you should see the size of my hands.

Believe it or not, I'd been in such bad shape that I actually got comparatively healthier on that diet. Over the course of a year, I lost about fifty pounds (don't you wish you could eat that much and lose fifty pounds?), my nosebleeds stopped, my blood pressure started coming down, and my cholesterol dove under 300, down to about 230, approaching what is considered the "normal" range. I was doing pretty well, and I was starting to feel better about myself.

Then a new, remarkable dynamic took hold. As I began to feel better about myself, my standards went up. I raised the bar higher in terms of what constituted acceptable health. And I knew instinctively that I wasn't going to get there on my brand of vegetarian diet.

I decided to try to be a vegan. For a person who hadn't even heard the term a year before, it was a giant step. Frankly, I didn't think I could do it. Eggs, cheese, butter, yogurt, and ice cream had become absolute staples of my vegetarian fare. I was definitely moving out of my comfort zone. But as long as I didn't have to tell anyone other than Willow Jeane about it, I was willing to fall on my face in the attempt.

Day by day, however, I discovered more and more foods that I could eat, and the surprising thing was that I enjoyed my vegan meals consistently. (Before I had turned vegetarian, I used to get a bad piece of meat from time to time, but I never met a stalk of asparagus I didn't like.) I could eat Chinese food, Thai food, Mexican food, Indian food, Italian food—all had dishes that could be made without animal products. There was a variety of grains—rice and barley and millet and couscous—around which I could organize my meals, and all kinds of organic fruits and vegetables at the produce market where I had begun to shop. For the first time in my life, I actually enjoyed shopping in a grocery store. And then there were all the new-fangled vegan products to which I had seldom paid attention before. There were high-protein foods such as tofu, tempeh, and seitan, and all the meat analogues that tasted remarkably like ham and bologna and hot dogs, but were made with soy and wheat.

It took me, therefore, about a year to make the full transition from meat-eater to vegan. In retrospect, I wish I had become vegan sooner. But we all have to do what feels comfortable to us, while at the same time challenging our-selves to reach an optimal state of health. I would personally recommend a pure vegetarian diet to anyone, and encour-age an immediate conversion. Nonetheless, if the thought of sudden change intimidates you, perhaps you'll prefer to gradually cut down on meat products, and gradually learn to prepare more vegetarian meals.

You might start with one vegetarian day per week, then work your way up toward seven. Just don't sell yourself short. It's not as hard as you might think to make a quick, or literally overnight, adjustment to a vegetarian or even to a vegan lifestyle. In fact, it's often easier to make a sudden shift than a gradual one, so that your taste buds can adapt to new sensations and leave the taste of meat and grease be-hind entirely. Once you adapt to low-fat vegetarian foods, you'll probably find that meats and fatty foods that used to appeal to you no longer do. If you continue eating those foods, even in diminished quantity, you may retain the craving for them. If you have high cholesterol, weight prob-lems, diabetes, or other health concerns, keep in mind that you can't expect palpable changes to your health, or to the way you look or feel, if you make only minor alterations to a meat-and-dairy-based diet. If you are a young, slender meat-eater without any known health problems, remember that a change to a vegetarian diet may not make you feel any different now. It's an investment in your future, in pre-venting atherosclerosis down the road, and in reversing the buildup of plaque in your arteries that has most likely al-ready begun without your knowledge.

What if the other members of your family eat meat, and you usually eat your meals together? While this could pre-sent difficulties, it could also present an opportunity. Explain to them why you want to make this change, and ask them to support you through the transition. Your family may want to try vegetarian meals together, or you may have to fix something separate for yourself. When your family members see how you're thriving on this diet, they may soon want to go vegetarian too. Ultimately, you can save their hearts as well as your own.

What if you're under eighteen, living with your parents, and they insist that you eat the meat they serve? This is a tough situation—one that arises often from the natural and healthy disinclination of many children and adolescents to eat animals—and I don't want to minimize how stressful it can potentially become. But understand that your parents are simply misinformed. They are making their demands on you with love in their hearts and all kinds of myths in their heads. It is your job to try to educate them. Give them books, teach them as well as you can. Ultimately, though, if they refuse to listen to reason, remember that no one—not even a misguided, loving parent—has the right to poison your body. Try not to compromise on that principle. You won't win the argument, though, by replacing meat with junk foods. Go shopping with your parents and insist that they provide you with whole, nutritious foods. For help and support, you might want to call an organization such as EarthSave International (see Bibliography), or contact a vegetarian friend in your community.

I am often struck by a phenomenon in the media: quite frequently, there is news of a "breakthrough" in medical understanding of the role of some nutrient in our diet. One day it might be the finding that cruciferous vegetables play an important role in preventing cancer; another might bring the news that antioxidant-rich foods such as raisins, sesame seeds, and green and orange vegetables prevent cholesterol from oxidizing and turning dangerous; or that genistein, found in soybeans, inhibits the growth of tumors; or that apple skin, red wine, and purple grape juice are all good for dilating blood vessels and protecting the heart; or that onions and garlic provide a world of health benefits—fighting viruses, cancer, high blood pressure, and cholesterol; or that fiber lowers serum cholesterol; or that saponins, a class of compounds found in fruits and vegetables, stimulate the immune system and may have antitumor properties. There is, simply, a never-ending stream of good news about vegetarian foods. In the words of Natalie Angier of the *New York Times,* "The truth is that the more researchers understand about the ingredients found in fruits, vegetables, beans, and herbs, the more impressed they are with the power of those compounds to retard the bodily breakdown that results in cancer and other chronic diseases." But you never hear any good news about meat. You never switch on the news to learn that a medical study at Harvard has revealed that roast beef boosts the immune system, or that fried chicken helps prevent arthritis, or that ham is good for the prostate. There's never a single encouraging news tidbit about veal, say, aiding the gonads. Nothing positive ever turns up even about the highly regarded *turkey escalopes fontina.* There's simply never anything health-enhancing that any researcher can uncover about flesh foods. Meanwhile, a torrent of revelations confirms the benefits of plant foods. Although it is rare for anybody in the media to note it, you've got to be blind not to see a pattern.

Take the case of homocysteine, an amino acid derived from the breakdown of another amino acid, methionine, present in greater proportion in animal than vegetable protein. In the early 1960s, a rare disease called homocystinuria was discovered in Ireland. Victims may suffer a variety of ailments, including mental retardation, but all cases are characterized by elevated levels of homocysteine in the blood and urine, and hardening of the arteries. This discovery led to the hypothesis that perhaps homocysteine, rather than cholesterol, is the active agent in breaking down the lining of arteries. Recently, evidence has mounted that indeed serum homocysteine levels mirror risk of cardiac arrest. Homocysteine is broken down by vitamin $B_6$ and folic acid, both abundantly present in plant foods. Proponents of the homocysteine hypothesis point to the ratio between methionine and vitamin $B_6$ in foods as the crucial factor for arterial health, finding this ratio worrisome in animal foods and ideal in fruits and vegetables. And so the debate in the medical community between the cholesterol model of arterial disease and the homocysteine model shakes out this way: those in the medical majority who emphasize the risk of elevated serum cholesterol as a cause of heart disease must by logic concede that the optimal diet is a low-fat, zero-cholesterol diet: a vegan diet. Those in the medical minority who by contrast emphasize the risk factor of elevated homocysteine in the blood must by logic concede that the optimal diet is the one lowest in methionine and highest in folic acid and vitamin $B_6$–a vegan diet. The scientific debate between the cholesterol model and the homocysteine model of heart disease essentially boils down to no more than an argument about which does the most damage: saturated fat and cholesterol from animal foods, or animal protein itself. In practical, dietary terms, it is a distinction without a difference.

If you decide to follow all the arrows and move to a vegetarian or vegan diet, you will most likely encounter some resistance from others who lack your insight or courage to change. Some people may say that you're a fool. Don't worry about it—you'll outlive them. Other vegetarian fools include Plato, Socrates, Einstein, Tolstoy, Thoreau, Emerson, Franklin, Pope, Newton, Pythagoras, Gandhi, Da Vinci, Voltaire, Milton, Darwin, Schweitzer, Shelley, Shaw, Paul Mc-Cartney, and, last but not least, Madonna. Some may say that you're too extreme—that you're better off just cutting down on meat products instead of going vegetarian. But if something's unhealthy for your body, by what logic would it be better to ingest a moderate amount of it than to eliminate it altogether? Some who are ignorant of the facts may tell you that you can't get enough protein on a vegetarian diet—but as we know, most Americans suffer from an unhealthy excess of protein. You will have absolutely no problem getting sufficient protein on a balanced vegetarian diet. Other naysayers may warn you that you're likely to become anemic. In fact, most vegetarians have very healthy hemoglobin levels; only those who eat a diet of junk foods and dairy products (which are iron-deficient) may run into problems. Some skeptics may bring up the cloudier matter of vitamin $B_{12}$. It's a fact that only animal foods contain substantial quantities of this vitamin. The human need for vitamin $B_{12}$ is minuscule—about 2 micrograms per day, and our bodies store the vitamin for a period of years. Vitamin $B_{12}$ is manufactured by bacteria and other one-celled organisms, and therefore our ancestors probably got plenty of it when they ate root vegetables and plants without washing all the soil off. Naturally, I don't suggest not washing your vegetables; there are plenty of easy ways for a vegan to obtain $B_{12}$. Some scientists believe that we get adequate levels of $B_{12}$ from intestinal bacteria and bacteria in the environment, but to be conservative, I recommend supplemental $B_{12}$. Many cereals, soy milks, and other packaged foods are enriched with $B_{12}$. Nutritional yeast and textured vegetable protein are also good sources. Finally, all multivitamins–including vegetarian formulas–contain more $B_{12}$ than you will ever need. So vitamin $B_{12}$ deficiency (which can lead to pernicious anemia) is nothing to worry about even on a strictly vegan diet–but, to be perfectly safe, simply enrich your diet with supplements. Nursing mothers should take particular care to do so.

Finally, there is what I consider the argument of last resort against vegetarianism. It is an argument that dismisses the facts in favor of supposition. Never mind the statistics about heart attacks and cancer, never mind that vegetarians tend to live longer than meat-eaters, never mind the obesity that is the common result of an animal-based diet, never mind all the environmental reasons for a diet that is plant-based–*humans were meant to be meat-eaters,* some plead. *We evolved as hunters. We have canine teeth. You can't fight Nature– we have blood lust.*

The reality, thankfully, is otherwise. We are not inexplicably doomed by Nature to a diet that destroys our bodies. Evolution created many carnivores, such as the lion, dog, wolf, and cat. They all have a short digestive system, roughly three times the length of their bodies, to facilitate the speedy removal of decaying flesh, which can poison the bloodstream if it lingers too long in the body. Carnivores also differ from herbivores in having acidic saliva and stomachs with large amounts of hydrochloric acid–useful in digesting flesh and bones. Animals that hunt at night and sleep by day don't need sweat glands and so don't perspire through their skin; instead, they sweat through their tongues. And carnivores of course have claws, powerful jaws, and long, sharp "canine" teeth to tear living flesh. They do not possess molars needed for grinding their food, or the enzyme ptyalin for predigesting grain.

How do humans compare in these regards? The answer is not new to science; it was given long ago by Plutarch, who pointed out that man "has no curved beak, no sharp talons or claws, no pointed teeth . . . on the contrary, by the smoothness of his teeth, the small capacity of his mouth, the softness of his tongue and the sluggishness of his digestive apparatus, Nature sternly forbids him to feed on flesh." Plutarch was right. Like our cousins the anthropoid apes, whose diet consists mostly of fruit and nuts, our digestive system is twelve times the length of our bodies (it takes meat five days to take this voyage and pass out of the body; vegetarian food, one to two days), our skin has pores for evaporation, and our stomach acid has roughly 5 percent the strength of the carnivores'. Obviously, we have neither claws nor powerful carnivorous jaws, but have molars for grinding and predigesting our grain. Like herbivorous animals, we have alkaline saliva and the enzyme ptyalin to predigest grain. The teeth we call our "canines" have only the name in common with the long, sharp, piercing teeth of dogs or tigers. If you don't believe me, try using your "canines" to tear into the living flesh of a moose. I have challenged many people to do so, and not one has come back with the moose in his mouth.

Do we have blood lust? Well, does the idea of tearing a chicken or a cow apart with your hands and teeth and sucking its warm blood appeal to you? People eat their meat packaged and disguised precisely because the reality of eating flesh disgusts most of us.

Maybe there's a reason for that.

CHAPTER NINE

# Going Home

I have been on the road for the last several years, traveling up to one hundred thousand miles a year, speaking to anyone who'll listen about the health benefits of a vegetarian diet and the dangers posed to our land and our bodies by chemical agriculture.

I've spoken in nearly every state, with one notable exception. Montana was never on my itinerary. I suppose that's at least partly because there's not a great demand for vegetarian speakers in Montana, but it's also the case that I wasn't real eager to go home. I love the state, and I miss my old friends there, yet something in my gut was telling me not to return, that I'd find it too painful.

I went back while writing this book, and saw what my gut was warning me about.

Family farming in the Montana that I knew is not just dying, as I had feared—it is dead. All the familiar small dairies, many with histories spanning several generations, have closed. I visited my old friend Harry Mitchell, who had once been the proprietor of the largest, most successful dairy farm in Montana, Ayrshire Dairy. (When I was a child, the only other dairy of comparable size in the state was the Lyman Dairy.) Today his farm is devoid of livestock and deathly quiet. If Harry Mitchell, the most hardworking, skillful, knowledgeable farmer you'd ever want to meet, can't run a dairy profitably today, no one can.

All the farmers and former farmers with whom I spoke had an edge of despair in their voices as they discussed the condition of agriculture in Montana and across the nation. There was no joy left in farming. Competing against agribusinesses, giant feedlots, and megadairies–all of which have taken every possible advantage of their size and rigged government policy to favor themselves–none of the family farmers truly had a chance. Government farm subsidies, often too complex for any single human to understand, have long tended to favor large-scale agriculture. Dairies in southern states, which don't have the expense of keeping their cows warm, have exploited their natural advantage over those in the northern states. The failures of chemical agriculture meanwhile have drawn most farmers deeper and deeper into a financial pit, as their soil has grown less productive. For all these reasons, more Montanan family farmers are throwing in the towel every week. Many are selling their land for housing developments or golf courses. Tourism is quickly replacing agriculture as the leading industry in the state. And the plight of Montana's small farmers is echoed across the land. When I sold my farm in 1983, there were about 1,250,000 full-time commercial family farms in America. Today about 400,000 remain. At this rate, the family farmer will be virtually extinct within a decade.

Family farmers are easier to lose than to replace. I would be a hypocrite if I claimed to feel unmitigated grief for the decline of dairies that, after all, yield a product that I now believe to be counterproductive to human health; but I do lament deeply the passing of a way of life, the rending of the fabric of community across rural America. And I feel for the small farmers who are losing out to the same high-tech, high-input, chemical means of production that is increasingly the bane of consumers, taxpayers, and the land itself.

With a lump in my throat, I headed back to the old family homestead. It was raining, and I trudged through the muddy soil around the fossilized remains of the sheds, granaries, scale houses, loading chutes, corrals, and feed bunks that I had once built. It was tough. Tough to feel that a lifetime of work and energy and heartbreak had gone into creating something that now is overgrown with weeds. Tough to realize that maybe if I had gone about it the right way, it would still be a productive, flourishing farm today.

I visited the cemetery where my parents and my brother are buried. My father's headstone is the size of a large refrigerator. The stone was rubbed smooth by buffalo that had brushed up against it for ages before cattle usurped them upon the land. My father had pointed the stone out to me when I was about fifteen. "You see that big old rock over there? That's what I want for my headstone." He never said another word about it, and neither did I. Thirty-five years later, when he died, I made sure his wish was carried out. It's one of the few things back home that I got right.

I looked up the fellows I used to play poker with. Of the other nine men who were all about my age (I am fifty-nine), four are dead (three of heart disease, one of emphysema), three live with heart disease, one has battled colon cancer, and another has survived cancer of the prostate. I'm the only one in good health. It seemed as if heart disease and cancer had visited practically every family I dropped in on. Everyone I spoke to was curious about my eating habits, but they were discreet. A pattern developed. Nobody wanted to ask me too many questions about my vegetarian diet in public, but whenever my friends cornered me alone, they pumped me for information. What do I have for dinner on a vegetarian diet? Fish? How do I get enough protein? My friends suffered from a lot of misinformation, but they knew something was seriously wrong with the way they were eating. Too many people were obese, too many were sick, too many had already died. The plague of the animal-based diet had wreaked havoc on their families and their community. They knew in their hearts that it was time to change. They just didn't know how.

In some, change inspires fear. What would happen to the economy, one friend challenged me, if I had my way and the nation went vegetarian? What would happen to all the jobs in the meat industry?

They would be lost, of course. Gone would be all the jobs in the slaughterhouses–the most dangerous jobs in America– as well as all the other foul jobs in meat processing, not to mention all the minimum wage jobs flipping burgers. They would be replaced by even more jobs–safer, cleaner, more satisfying, and probably better-paying jobs–in the production and selling of organic, healthy, plant-based products. The savings in medical costs attributable to meat consumption, estimated at $28 to $61 billion annually, would be plowed back into our economy and boost its productivity enormously.

Organic farming is labor-intensive, and more conducive to small farming operations than large. That is why the loss of a generation of family farmers troubles me greatly. We need skilled farmers to help sustain the transition to small-scale, organic agriculture that just happens to be the fastest-growing segment of the farm economy today. And organic agriculture thrives without imposing hidden costs on tax-payers the way the chicken and hog and cattle operations do when their waste products run off into our waterways. I think of the words of my friend Fred Kirschenmann, who runs a prosperous organic farm in North Dakota: "My neighbors outproduce me in just about every respect but one," Fred says. "Net profit." He has far lower input costs than the chemical farmers, and consumers wisely are willing to pay more for his goods.

The change is underway. I paid a visit to the largest commercial supermarket in Great Falls. I could hardly believe my eyes. Soy milk and rice milk on the shelves. Soy hot dogs, veggie burgers, tofu, and seitan. And I found vegetarian entrees in all the restaurants I sampled. It's not hard anymore to be a vegetarian in America. If it can be done in Great Falls, it can be done anywhere.

The question we must ask ourselves as a culture is whether we want to embrace the change that must come, or resist it. Are we so attached to the dietary fallacies with which we were raised, so afraid to counter the arbitrary laws of eating taught to us in childhood by our misinformed parents, that we cannot alter the course they set us on, even if it leads to our own ruin? Does the prospect of standing apart or encountering ridicule scare us even from saving ourselves?

That prospect intimidated me once, and I can only wonder now what I was frightened of. It's hard to imagine, now that I'm a hundred thirty pounds lighter, infinitely healthier, more full of life and energy, much happier. Now that I have vegetarian friends wherever I go, and feel part of a movement that is not so much political as it is a march of the human heart. Now that I understand how much is at stake. Now that I've come to relish shaking people up.

I would love to see the meat industry and the pesticide industry shaken up, too. I would love to see feedlots close and factory farming end. I would love to see more families return to the land, grow crops for our own species, and raise them organically. I would love to see farm communities revive. I would love to know that I've wandered into my nation's heartland by the sweet smell of grain and not the forbidding smell of excrement.

I can no longer fathom what there is to be afraid of, except the status quo.

How do we want, in the end, to measure the lives we have led? We could measure them, of course, according to how much money and how many material possessions we've accumulated. But, in the words made famous by a great American play, you can't take it with you.

Or we could ask ourselves: have we done all that we could for the generations to come? Are there more trees now than there were when we were born? Is the air fresher? Is the water cleaner? Is there more good, rich farmland? Are there more birds in the sky, more fish in the sea? Are there more animals in the wild? Are people leading longer, healthier lives? Is there less hunger? Is there less disease and suffering? Is the world a more peaceful place?

When you can't take it with you, all that really matters is what you leave behind.

# ENDNOTES

## Chapter One: How to Tell the Truth and Get in Trouble

PAGE

12    *$2.4-billion-a-year industry:* Blakeslee, Sandra, "Fear Prompts Look at Rendering," *New York Times,* March 11, 1997, p. B8.

12    *six or seven million dogs and cats:* Ibid.

12    *two hundred tons of euthanized cats and dogs:* Ibid.

12    *In 1995, five million tons:* Dr. Fred Bisplinghoff, testimony before USDA/APHIS and FDA/CVM Symposium on TSEs, May 13 and 14, 1996.

13    *About 75 percent of the ninety million beef cattle:* Mulvarey, Kienan, "Mad Cows and the Colonies," *E: The Environmental Magazine,* July/August 1996, vol. VII, no. 4, p. 38.

13    *1.6 million tons of livestock wastes:* Tharp., C., and W. P. Miller, "Poultry Litter Practices of Arkansas Poultry Producers," USDA, 1994 (Sustainable Agriculture Research and Education Project AS92-1), cited in Haapapuro, Eric R., et al., "Animal Waste Used as Livestock Feed: Dangers to Human Health," Physicians Committee for Responsible Medicine review, 1997, p. 1.

13    *over fifty tons of chicken litter:* Ibid., p. 2.

13    *One Arkansas cattle farmer:* Satchell, Mitchell, and Stephen J. Hedges, "The Next Bad Beef Scandal," *U.S. News & World Report,* September 1, 1997, p. 22.

13    *causes the death of nine thousand Americans a year:* Agriculture Department statistic, cited in Fox, Nicols, "Safe Food? Not Yet," *New York Times,* January 30, 1997, p. A21.

13    *80 percent of food poisonings:* O'Connor, Amy, "8 Nutritional Myths," *Vegetarian Times,* July 1997, p. 80.

13    *now we can also be virtually certain:* Collinge, John, et al., "Spongiform Encephalopathies: A Common Agent for BSE and vCJD," *Nature,* October 2, 1997, pp. 449–50.

14    *"Right now," I explained:* The Oprah Winfrey Show, April 16, 1996.

14    *"It has just stopped me cold . . .":* Ibid.

15    *Pointing to a drop in the cattle futures market:* "Oprah Moves World Markets," AP, April 17, 1996.

15    *Controversy even erupted in nineteenth-century Hungary:* Robbins, John, *Reclaiming Our Health* (Tiburon, Calif.: H. J. Kramer, 1996), pp. 15–16.

15    *Thirteen states have Food Disparagement laws:* "Free Speech About Food," *New York Times* editorial, January 19, 1998, p. A14.

15    *emu ranchers against the Honda Motor Company:* Cropper, Carol

# ENDNOTES

Marie, "Texas and Arkansas Emu Ranchers Sue Honda Over a TV Spot They Say Disparages Their Birds," *New York Times,* November 6, 1997, p. C6.

16 *the Beef Promotion Council pulled over six hundred thousand dollars':* "Oprah Causes Beef Industry Flap," *Meat Processing,* June 1996, p. 8, cited in Rampton, Sheldon, and John Stauber, *Mad Cow U.S.A.: Could the Nightmare Happen Here?* (Monroe, Maine: Common Courage Press, 1997), p. 21.

16 *$3-billion-a-year industry:* Pressley, Sue Anne, "Testing a New Brand of Libel Law," *Washington Post,* January 17, 1998, p. A12.

16 *Twenty-five percent of U.S. cattle:* Ibid.

17 *no "red carpet rollouts,":* Verhovek, Sam Howe, "Talk of the Town: Burgers v. Oprah," *New York Times,* January 21, 1998, p. A10.

18 *"the most painful thing I've ever experienced,":* Chandler, Chip, "Oprah: Lawsuit Is 'Most Painful,'" *Amarillo Globe-News,* February 5, 1998, p. 1A.

18 *"never done a malicious act,":* Ibid.

19 *"If you appeared on a national talk show,":* Chandler, Chip, "Witness Blames Show for Drop in Markets," *Amarillo Globe-News,* February 11, 1998, p. 2A.

## Chapter Two: The Simple Facts

PAGE

21 *About 80 percent of pesticides:* Hitchcox, Lee, *Long Life Now* (Berkeley, Calif.: Celestial Hearts, 1996) p. 59.

21 *According to a 1975 study:* "Environmental Quality–1975," The Sixth Annual Report of the Council on Environmental Quality, Washington, D.C., December 1975, p. 375; cited in John Robbins, *Diet for a New America* (Walpole, N.H.: Stillpoint Publishing, 1987), p. 343.

22 only 1 to 2 percent *of the national average: New England Journal of Medicine,* March 26, 1981, cited in Robbins, op. cit., p. 345.

22 *Today, that figure is one in three:* Kushi, Michio, *The Cancer Prevention Diet* (New York: St. Martin's Press, 1994), p. 3.

22 *The evidence mounts that farmers:* Krebs, A. V., *The Corporate Reapers* (Washington, D.C.: Essential Books, 1991), p. 85. Krebs cites, for example, a 32 percent greater cancer risk for Iowa farmers compared to nonfarmers, and a 44 percent greater leukemia risk in Nebraska for farmers compared to nonfarmers.

23 *One out of every two Americans:* Whitaker, Julian, *Reversing Heart Disease* (New York: Warner Books, 1985), pp. 3–4.

24 *"Death of heart disease . . .":* Ibid., p. 4.

24 *A study of mortality following a major earthquake in Athens:* Tricholpoulos, Dimitrios, "Psychological Fitness and Fatal Heart Attack: The Athens Earthquake Natural Experiment," *Lancet,* 1:443, 1983.

24 *"Recent research shows . . .":* Ornish, Dean, *Dr. Dean Ornish's Program for Reversing Heart Disease* (New York: Ballantine Books, 1990), p. 76.

25 *But in fact the death rate from heart disease fell:* Whitaker, op. cit., pp. 60–62.

25    *"A study in 1970 . . .":* Keys, A. (ed.), "Coronary Heart Disease in Seven Countries," American Heart Association Monograph No. 29, *Circulation,* 41, Supplement 1, 1970, p. 211; Keys, A. (ed.), "Seven Countries–A Multivariate Analysis of Death and Coronary Heart Disease in Ten Years" (Cambridge: Harvard University Press), 1980, cited in Robbins, op. cit., p. 212.

26    *"An extraordinary study conducted in the mid-1970's":* Robbins, op. cit., p. 215; Cox, Peter, *Why You Don't Need Meat* (London: Bloomsbury Publishing, 1992), pp. 3–6.

26    *"A study published in 1988 . . .":* Cox, op. cit., p. 8.

26    *"A massive population study known as the China Health Project . . .":* The work of T. Colin Campbell has been widely reported on. It was cited, for example, in Cox, op. cit., pp. 9–10.

26    *"A study in Germany . . .":* Food Chemical News, September 21, 1992, p. 10.

26    *"vegans have cholesterol levels . . .":* Marcus, Erik, *Vegan: The New Ethics of Eating* (Ithaca, N.Y.: McBooks Press, 1997), pp. 10, 14.

26    *"A vegetarian diet can prevent . . .": Journal of the American Medical Association,* vol. 176, no. 9, June 3, 1961, p. 806, cited in Robbins, op. cit., p. 247.

27    *they have not found a single person to have a heart attack:* Whitaker, op. cit., p. 114; Marcus, op. cit., p. 10; Ornish, op. cit., p. 268.

28    *"among persons examined less than 2 years before their death . . .":* Gordon, Tavia, and William B. Kannel, "Premature Mortality from Coronary Heart Disease: The Framingham Study," *Journal of the American Medical Asociation,* vol. 215, no. 10, March 8, 1971, p. 1621.

28    *"a disease which can be silent even in the most dangerous form":* Ibid., p. 1624.

28    *A study in Italy:* Descovich, G. C., "Multicentre Study of Soybean Protein Diet for Outpatient Hypercholesterolaemic Patients," *Lancet,* 2:709, 1980.

29    *"For some reason there is widespread belief . . .":* Whitaker, op. cit., p. 10.

29    *their rate of heart disease increases as much as tenfold:* Ibid., p. 12.

30    *"Even though these people will have a lower risk . . . ":* McDougall, John A., *The McDougall Program: 12 Days to Dynamic Health* (New York: Penguin Books, 1990), p. 407.

30    *"After only one year . . .":* Ornish, op. cit., p. 19.

31    *A major study of 780 heart patients:* Whitaker, op. cit., p. 25.

31    *damage can occur to many of the body's vital organs:* Ibid., pp. 36–37.

31    *The German Cancer Research Center:* Frentzel-Beyme, R., et al., "Mortality among German Vegetarians: First Results After Five Years of Follow-up," *Nutrition and Cancer,* 11 (2), 1988, pp. 117–26, cited in Cox, op. cit., p. 8.

31    *The aforementioned study:* Kushi, op. cit., p. 240.

31    *a ten-year study of over 120,000 Japanese men:* Ibid.

31    *This study may have been:* Allen, N. E., Appleby, P. N., Davey, G.K., and Key, T. J., "Hormones and Diet: low insuline-like growth factor-I but normal

bioavailable androgens in vegan men," *British Journal of Cancer,* 2000:83: 95–97.

31    *"Populations on a high-meat, high-fat diet are more likely . . .": Science,* February 1974, cited in Robbins, op. cit., p. 253.

32    *"Risks of beef, pork, and chicken . . .": Journal of the National Cancer Institute,* December 1973, p. 1771, cited in Robbins, op. cit., p. 254.

32    *a thirty-six-country study:* Kushi, op. cit., p. 241.

32    *Numerous animal studies have shown:* Kradjian, Robert, *Save Yourself from Breast Cancer* (Berkeley, Calif.: Berkeley Publishing Group, 1994), pp. 51–52.

32    *Worldwide epidemiological evidence also reveals:* Ibid., p. 44.

32    *breast cancer in that country has shot up:* Ibid., p. 46.

33    *A massive Japanese study documented:* Hirayama, T., conference on Breast Cancer and Diet, U.S.–Japan Cooperative Cancer Research Program, Seattle, Washington, March 14–15, 1977, cited in Robbins, op. cit., p. 264.

33    *Not surprisingly, in the United States, Seventh-Day Adventist women:* Kushi, op. cit., p. 226.

33    *A 1989 Harvard study:* Ibid., p. 228.

33    *Finally, the less-than-radical National Academy of Sciences:* Ibid., p. 241.

33    *$40 billion annually:* Klein, Richard, "Dieting Dangerously," *New York Times,* July 14, 1997, p. A15.

33    *believe it or not, 25 percent more calories:* Cox, op. cit., p. 9.

34    *comparing cultures with different diets:* Ibid., p. 153; Robbins, op. cit., pp. 193–94.

34    *A study of 1,600 women:* Cox, op. cit., p. 153.

35    *half the risk of developing diabetes:* Snowdon, D. A., and R. L. Phillips, "Does a Vegetarian Diet Reduce the Occurrence of Diabetes?" *American Journal of Public Health,* 75, 1985, pp. 507–12, cited in Cox, op. cit., p. 138.

35    *required 73 percent less insulin therapy:* Anderson, J. W., "Plant Fiber and Blood Pressure," *Annals of Internal Medicine,* 98, 1983, pp. 842–46, cited in Cox, op. cit., p. 141.

35    *diabetes "is rare or nonexistent":* Robbins, op. cit., p. 277.

36    *One study published more than twenty years ago:* Sacks, F. M., et al., "Plasma Lipids and Lipoproteins in Vegetarians and Controls," *New England Journal of Medicine, 292,* 1975, pp. 1148–51, cited in Cox, op. cit., p. 121.

36    *a particularly cruel one:* Donaldson, A. N., "The Relation of Protein Foods to Hypertension," *Californian and Western Medicine,* 24, 1926, p. 328, cited in Cox, op. cit., p. 120.

36    *The benefits of a low-fat vegetarian diet:* see Barnard, Neal, *Eat Right, Live Longer* (New York: Crown Publishing, 1995); Robbins, op. cit.; Cox, op. cit; McDougall, op. cit.; Marcus, op. cit.

36    *Despite myths to the contrary:* Robbins, op. cit., pp. 299–300.

37    *The same-size serving of chicken:* McDougall, op. cit., p. 49. Cholesterol figures for pork, trout, and turkey are from the same source.

37    *More than 90 percent of chickens are raised on factory farms:* Jim Mason,

"Fowling the Waters," *E: The Environmental Magazine,* September/October 1995, p. 33.

38     *more than 99 percent of broiler carcasses:* Fox, Nichols, "Safe Food? Not Yet," *New York Times,* January 30, 1997, p. A21.

38     *30 percent of chicken consumed in America is contaminated:* Smith De-Waal, Caroline, "Playing Chicken: The Human Cost of Inadequate Regulation of the Poultry Industry," Center for Science in the Public Interest, March 1996, p. 4; Haapapuro, Eric R., et al., op. cit., p. 1.

38     *and 70 to 90 percent with another deadly pathogen, campylobacter:* Burros, Marian, "Health Concerns Mounting Over Bacteria in Chickens," *New York Times,* October 20, 1997, p. A1.

38     *campylobacter causes two hundred to eight hundred deaths a year:* Ibid.

38     *two thousand cases per year of a rare paralytic disease:* Ibid.

38     *the bacterium has proved increasingly resistant:* Ibid., pp. A1, A10.

38     *up to 25 percent of chickens on the inspection line:* Government Accountability Project, "Fighting Filth on the Kill Floor: A Matter of Life and Death for America's Families," November 9, 1995, p. 4.

38     *individual chicken inspectors examine:* Statement of John Harmon, Director, "Building a Scientific, Risk-Based Meat and Poultry Inspection System," *Food and Agricultural Issues,* General Accounting Office, March 16, 1993, GAO/T-RCED-93-22.

38     *contaminated chicken still manages to kill at least one thousand Americans:* Behar, Richard, and Michael Kramer, "Something Smells Fowl," *Time,* October 17, 1994, pp. 42–44.

39     *A thorough 1992* Consumer Reports *study:* "Is Our Fish Fit to Eat?" *Consumer Reports,* February 1992, pp. 103–14.

39     *The Centers for Disease Control reports:* Williams, Gurney III, "What's Wrong with Fish?" *Vegetarian Times,* August 1995.

39     *"exceeded the upper limits of our test method,"* Consumer Reports, February 1992, p. 104.

39     *dead for two weeks or more:* Ibid.

39     *upwards of 30 percent of fish:* Ibid., p. 103.

40     *PCBs in 43 percent of salmon:* Ibid., February 1992, p. 112.

40     *"pregnant women or women who expect to become pregnant":* Ibid., p. 106.

40     *women who ate fish from Lake Michigan:* Jacobson, Joseph L., and Jacobson, Sandra W., "Intellectual Impairment in Children Exposed to Polychlorinated Biphenyls in Utero," *New England Journal of Medicine,* September 12, 1996, vol. 335, no. 11, pp. 783–89.

42     *It takes sixteen pounds of grain:* Lappé, Frances Moore, *Diet for a Small Planet–Revised Tenth Anniversary Edition* (New York: Ballantine Books, 1982), p. 9.

41     *we forfeit 90 percent of the original protein:* James, Helen, "Meat and World Hunger," *Veggie Singles News,* autumn 1997, p. 11.

# ENDNOTES

42    *When you consider that an acre of fertile land: Soil and Water,* vol. 38, University of California Cooperative Extension.

42    *By far the greater share of that population growth:* Crossette, Barbara, "How to Fix a Crowded World: Add People," *New York Times,* November 2, 1997, sect. 4, pp. 1, 3.

42    *A recent report of the Worldwatch Institute:* Brown, Lester, et al., *Vital Signs: 1994* (Washington, D.C.: Worldwatch Institute, 1994).

43    *the hijacking of agricultural systems in hungry countries:* Lappé, Frances Moore, and Joseph Collins, *Food First* (Boston: Houghton Mifflin, 1977).

43    *a million acres of farmland will be lost:* Goldberg, Carey, "Alarm Bells Sounding as Suburbs Gobble Up California's Richest Farmland," *New York Times,* June 20, 1996, p. A10.

43    *the valley won't even be able to feed itself:* Ibid.

44    *with the single proviso:* Durning, Alan B., "Fat of the Land," Worldwatch Institute Report, vol. 4, no. 3, May/June 1991, p. 12.

44    *are considered commercially extinct:* Safina, Carl, "The World's Imperiled Fish," Scientific American, vol. 273, no. 5, November 1995, p. 48.

44    *In 1994, fishing enterprises worldwide:* Ibid., p. 50; Brown et al., op. cit., p. 32.

45    *Since the 1970s, food production of the basic grains:* Lappé, Frances Moore, *Diet for a Small Planet—Twenty Years Later* (New York: Ballantine Books, 1992), p. xvii.

45    *"While 70 per cent of the protein . . .":* Cox, op. cit., p. 9.

## Chapter Four: From the Farm to the Capital

PAGE

72    *637,666,000 pounds of the synthetic poisons:* Carson, Rachel, *Silent Spring* (Boston: Houghton Mifflin, 1962, 1994), p. 17. The statistic is from 1960.

72    *Today, as Vice President Gore points out:* Gore, Albert, Introduction to Carson, op. cit., p. xix.

73    *"This pollution is for the most part . . .":* Carson, op. cit., p. 6.

80    *livestock outnumber humans on the planet:* James, Helen, op. cit., p. 11.

80    *I'd learned that about 50 percent of our water usage:* Lappé, Frances Moore, *Diet for a Small Planet—Revised Tenth Anniversary Edition,* (New York: Ballantine Books, 1982), p. 10.

80    *I'd learned that we were losing topsoil at a rate:* Hur, Robin, "Six Inches from Starvation: How and Why America's Topsoil Is Disappearing," *Vegetarian Times,* March 1985, pp. 45–47.

## Chapter Five: Mad Cows and Bureaucrats

PAGE

85    *His prion theory had been influenced:* Rhodes, Richard, *Deadly Feasts* (New York: Simon & Schuster, 1997), pp. 121–23, 160–62. Rhodes attacks

Prusiner for trying to "claim priority for work other people had already done," p. 205.

85    *scrapie-infected brains had retained their ability:* Prusiner, Stanley B., "The Prion Diseases," *Scientific American,* January 1995, p. 49.

85    *in all mammals tested—including humans:* Ibid.

85    *"the scrapie protein propagates itself . . .":* Ibid., p. 52.

86    *"Goats and sheep . . .":* Rhodes, op. cit., p. 121.

88    *Cattle injected with U.S. strains of scrapie:* "U.S. Takes Step to Avoid Mad Cow Disease," Reuters, September 23, 1997, citing Dr. Paul Brown of the National Institute of Neurological Disorders and Stroke, Bethesda, Maryland.

88    *Microbiologist Richard Lacey:* Lacey, Richard, *Mad Cow Disease: The History of BSE in Britain* ( Jersey, Channel Islands: Cipsela Publications, Ltd., 1994).

89    *"But why was only half the market value . . .":* Ibid., p. 60.

89    *Over two thousand confirmed cases:* This and succeeding facts about BSE in Great Britain, unless otherwise noted, are gleaned from Lacey, op. cit.

90    *"because the possibility . . .":* Southwood, R., Report of the Working Party on Bovine Spongiform Encephalopathy, 1989, General Conclusions, 9.3, cited in Lacey, op. cit., p. 68.

90    *two further half-measures to meet the crisis:* Lacey, op. cit., pp. 79-83.

91    *predicting that the disease would soon die out:* Lacey, op. cit. p. 127.

91    *"it would have no significance for public health":* Ministry of Agriculture News Release, March 27, 1992, cited in Lacey, op. cit., p. 127.

92    *To her credit, she refused to take a bite:* Rampton, Sheldon, and John Stauber, *Mad Cow U.S.A.: Could the Nightmare Happen Here?* (Monroe, Maine: Common Courage Press, 1997), p. 131.

92    *"It was in September 1993 . . .":* Lacey, op. cit., pp. 164–65.

93    *about 10 percent of animals from infected herds:* Lacey, Richard, {Mad Cow Disease Update," insert to *Mad Cow Disease: The History of BSE in Britain.*

93    *averaging twenty-seven years old:* Marcus, Erik, *Vegan: The New Ethics of Eating* (Ithaca, N.Y.: McBooks Press, 1997) p. 74; Hawkes, Nigel, "Subtle Differences Led Scientists to Link BSE with Humans," *The Times* (London), March 21, 1996, p. 3.

94    *"the Government Surveillance Unit in Edinburgh . . .":* Rampton and Stauber, op. cit., p. 183.

94    *Ireland stepped up protections:* Ibid., p. 13.

95    *The brain pathology of those who succumbed:* Rampton and Stauber, op. cit., pp. 179–80; Brown Paul, "Bovine Spongiform Encephalopathy and Creutzfeldt-Jakob Disease," *British Medical Journal,* vol. 312, no. 7034, March 30, 1996, pp. 790–91.

95    *a new biochemical test for prions:* Collinge, John, et al., "Molecular Analysis of Prion Strain Variation and the Aetiology of 'New Variant' CJD," *Nature,* October 24, 1996, p. 685.

95    *proved the link conclusively:* Collinge, John, et al., "Spongiform En-

ENDNOTES

cephalopathies: A Common Agent for BSE and vCJD," *Nature,* October 2, 1997, pp. 449–50.

96 *at least 750,000 cattle:* Anderson, R. M., et al., "Transmission Dynamics and Epidemiology of BSE in British Cattle," *Nature,* August 29, 1996, p. 779.

96 *Some 350,000 tons of meat: UK NEWS,* August 25, 1997.

97 *A report in the* New England Journal of Medicine: "Demonstration of the Transmissible Agent in Tissue from a Pregnant Woman with Creutzfeldt-Jakob Disease," Tamai, Yoichi, et al., *New England Journal of Medicine,* vol. 327, no. 9, August 27, 1992, p. 649.

97 *two hundred thousand British deaths beginning:* Rhodes, op. cit., p. 222.

98 *An FDA survey:* Center for Veterinary Medicine, Food and Drug Administration, "Report of Findings of Directed Inspections of Sheep Rendering Facilities," January 1993, p. 1, cited in Rampton and Stauber, op. cit., p. 150.

98 *an Agriculture Department survey in 1997:* "Hamburger Helper? USDA Reports Spinal Cord Bits in Ground Beef," AP, February 21, 1997.

100 *three of them had actually died of CJD: Neurology,* 1989, 39 (1): pp. 76–79.

100 *Also shockingly high is the number of CJD cases:* Beil, Laura "Texas Deaths Probed as 'Mad-Cow Disease,'" *San Francisco Examiner,* June 14, 1997, p. A-10.

100 *eight cases of CJD have been diagnosed:* Conversations between Glen Merzer and Julie Rawlings, Texas Department of Health, August 25, 1997, and November 3, 1997.

100 *a pig injected with BSE:* Hansen, Michael, "The Reasons Why FDA's Feed Rule Won't Protect Us from BSE," *Genetic Engineering News,* July 1997, p. 4.

100 *bovine blood meal has been excluded:* Ibid.

**Chapter Six: Biotech Bullies**

PAGE

102 *a majority of consumers:* Galloway, Jennifer A., "Survey: rBGH Still Scares Consumers," *Wisconsin State Journal,* January 26, 1996, p. 14. According to a University of Wisconsin study cited here, 53.8 percent of consumers have a poor overall opinion of rBGH.

103 *at least fourteen of the eight thousand individuals:* Davis, David, "Growing Pains," *L.A. Weekly,* March 21–27, 1997, pp. 23–30.

104 *The experience of John Kurtz: "Fastrack" Product Showcase,* Conklin corporate newsletter, vol. 62, pp. 1–4. All data on Kurtz's experience is from this source.

105 *left a lot of dairy farmers who used rBGH struggling to explain:* "Dairy Farmers Quit Use of Controversial Hormone," Wisconsin Farmers Union News Release, October 7, 1995.

105   *As one such farm family reported:* Knox, Paul, Martha Knox, and Joshua Knox, *Dairy Today,* August 1996, p. 4.

105   *"even their shoulder blades had a ripple effect . . .":* Kurtz, John, quoted in "Fastrack" Product Showcase, Conklin corporate newsletter, vol. 62, p. 2.

107   *Florida . . . became a milk-importing state:* Fritsch, Peter, and Scott Kilman, *Dow Jones News,* August 16, 1996, 5:04 A.M.

107   *When Monsanto faced accusations in the press:* "Monsanto Suffers Setback," *Frank* magazine, October 9, 1995; *FAIR* magazine, May/June 1995, pp. 19–20; Fritsch and Kilman, op. cit.

108   *"underwritten joint promotional campaigns . . .":* Krug, Bruce, coordinator of New York Farmers Union, quoted in BGH Report, *Rural Vermont,* November 1995, pp. 14–15.

108   *As one farmer reported:* Livingston, Jay, quoted in BGH Report, *Rural Vermont,* November 1995, p. 15.

108   *Currently the drug is used in only about 3 percent:* Conversation between Glen Merzer and Ronnie Cummins, Director, Pure Food Campaign, October 21, 1997.

108   *As the politically neutral Dow Jones News reported:* August 16, 1996, 6 A.M.

109   *Cows injected with rBGH have significantly higher incidence:* "BGH Problems Explode," Wisconsin Farmers Union News Release, March 14, 1995; Lambrecht, Bill, "Spoiling for Label Battle," *St. Louis Post-Dispatch,* January 28, 1990; *Rural Vermont,* November 1995, p. 3; Chelimsky, Eleanor, Assistant Comptroller General, letter to Health and Human Services Secretary Donna E. Shalala, March 2, 1993; Millstone, Erik, Eric Brunner, and Jan White, *Nature,* vol. 371, no. 6499, October 20, 1994, pp. 647–48.

110   *63 percent had detectable residues of antibiotics:* Kaneene, John B., and Miller, RoseAnn, "Description and evaluation of the influence of veterinary presence on the use of antibiotics and sulfonamides in dairy herds," *Journal of American Veterinary Medical Association,* vol. 201, no. 1, July 1, 1992, p. 68.

110   *A 1988 Illinois survey found that 58 percent:* August 1992 GAO report, "FDA Strategy Needed to Address Animal Drug Residues in Milk," cited in letter from Michael Hansen, Consumers Union, to Jerry Mande, Office of the Commissioner, FDA, May 24, 1993.

111   *"weaker than our so-called enemies":* Lappé, Marc, *When Antibiotics Fail* (Berkeley, Calif.: North Atlantic Books, 1986), p. xii.

111   *"Modern pharmaceuticals cannot begin . . .":* Ibid.

111   *the FDA has not investigated:* Montague, Peter, *Rachel's Hazardous Waste News,* #382, March 24, 1994.

111   *milk-fat concentrations in rBGH-treated cows:* Baer, et al., *Journal of Dairy Science,* 72:1424–34, 1989; Epstein, *International Journal of Health Services,* 20:73–84, 1990; Mepham, *Journal of the Royal Society of Medicine,* 85:736–39, 1992.

112   *IGF-1 levels of the milk of rBGH-treated cows:* Juskevich, Judith C.,

# ENDNOTES

and C. Greg Guyer, "BGH: Human Food Safety Evaluation," *Science,* 249:875–84, August 24, 1990; Prosser et al., *Journal of Dairy Research,* 56:17–26, 1989; Hansen, letter to Mande, op. cit.

112   *Similar increases in IGF-1 are also found:* National Institutes of Health, Technology Assessment Conference Statement on Bovine Somatotropin, *Journal of the American Medical Association,* 265, 1991, 1423–25.

112   *acknowledged a 500 percent elevation: Rachel's Environmental & Health Weekly,* #454, August 10, 1995.

112   *suspect it may play a role:* "Breast Cancer," Harris, Jay R., et al., *New England Journal of Medicine,* vol. 327, no. 7, 1992, pp. 473–80; Lippman, Mark E., "The Development of Biological Therapies for Breast Cancer," *Science,* 259: January 19, 1993, 631–32.

112   *A study of the effect of IGF-1 on the growth of rats:* Juskevich and Guyer, op. cit.

112   *Critics of the study:* Hansen, letter to Mande, op. cit.

113   *"Armed with the knowledge . . .":* Cohen, Robert, paper presented to the FDA on April 21, 1995, as a result of a citizen petition filed by Cohen.

113   *approximately three-quarters of consumers:* Galloway, op. cit.

114   *favored in various surveys by 80 to 98 percent of consumers:* Hansen, Michael K., testimony before the joint meeting of the Food Advisory Committee and the Veterinary Medicine Advisory Committee on whether to label milk from rBGH-treated cows, May 6, 1993.

114   *milk sales throughout the nation dropped dramatically: Bi Weekly Reader,* Omaha, Nebraska, November 9, 1994.

115   *"mandatory labeling of milk products":* International Dairy Foods Association News Release, April 25, 1994.

116   *suing a small, family-owned dairy in Waco:* Cummins, Ronnie, "rBGH and Biotech Foods Fight Continues," *Pure Food Campaign Newsletter,* November 7, 1994; *Rachel's Hazardous Waste News,* #382, March 24, 1994.

116   *three top-level officials of the FDA involved in formulating:* Schneider, Keith, "Question Is Raised on Hormone Maker's Ties to FDA Aides," *New York Times,* April 18, 1994, p. A9.

118   *costing Monsanto $10 million a year:* Stodghill II, Ron, "So Shall Monsanto Reap?" *BusinessWeek,* April 1, 1996, p. 67.

## Chapter Seven: Bovine Planet

PAGE

123   *We are losing precious rain forest:* Rainforest Action Network fact sheet, 1997.

124   *"An estimated eighty-five percent . . .":* Fox, Michael, *Agricide: The Hidden Crisis That Affects Us All* (New York: Schocken Books, 1986), pp. 50–51.

124   *About one-third of the annual increase:* Rifkin, Jeremy, *Beyond Beef: The Rise and Fall of the Cattle Culture* (New York: Plume, 1992), p. 224.

125　*"It now takes the equivalent of a gallon of gasoline . . .":* Ibid., p. 225.

126　*even the least efficient plant food ,. . . :* Roller, W. L., H. M. Keener, and R. D. Kline, "Energy Costs of Livestock Production" (St. Joseph, Mich.: American Society of Agricultural Engineers, June 1975), paper no. 75-4042, cited in Mason, Jim, and Peter Singer, *Animal Factories* (New York: Crown Publishers, 1990), p. 116 and Robbins, John, *Diet for a New America* (Walpole, N.H.: Stillpoint Publishing, 1987), p. 376.

127　*150 trillion quarts of methane gas:* Jacobs, Lynn, *Waste of the West* (Tucson: Lynn Jacobs, 1991), p. 146.

127　*Every cow emits up to 400 quarts:* Ibid.

127　*responsible for adding millions of tons of methane:* Rifkin, op. cit., p. 226.

127　*methane content of the atmosphere has doubled:* Jacobs, op. cit., p. 146.

128　*Dust storms have been linked to livestock grazing:* Ibid.

128　*"This damage is so prevalent . . .":* Wuerthner, George, "Public Lands Grazing–The Real Costs," *Earth First! The Radical Environmental Journal,* August 1, 1989.

128　*increase water temperatures by ten degrees or more:* Jacobs, op. cit., p. 85.

128　*Feedlot wastes can be several hundred times more concentrated:* Robbins, *op. cit.,* p. 373.

129　*On a typical feedlot:* Rifkin, op. cit., p. 221.

129　*a waste problem equal to that of the largest American cities:* Robbins, *op. cit.,* p. 372.

129　*ten times as much water pollution in America:* Robbins, *Ibid.,* p. 373.

129　*by a factor of one hundred and thirty:* "Animal Waste Pollution in America: An Emerging National Problem," report of the Minority Staff of the U.S. Senate Committee on Agriculture, Nutrition, and Forestry, December 1997, p. 1.

129　*thousands of cattle carcasses:* Jacobs, op. cit., p. 5.

130　*bacteria in the New River:* Barker, Rodney, *And the Waters Turned to Blood* (New York: Simon & Schuster, 1997), p. 237.

131　*from Delaware Bay to the Gulf of Mexico:* Ibid., p. 322.

131　*tributaries of Chesapeake Bay:* Cushman, John A., Jr., "Another Waterway Is Closed in Maryland," *New York Times,* September 15, 1997, p. A8.

131　*"In the Northwest . . .":* Jacobs, op. cit., p. 215.

132　*about 70 percent of the water:* Ibid.

132　*the water required to produce* just ten pounds of steak*:* Lappé, *Diet for a Small Planet–Revised Tenth Anniversary Edition,* p. 76.

133　*Nearly half the grain-fed cattle:* Rifkin, op. cit., p. 219.

133　*Over the last four decades:* Ibid.

133　*Our tax dollars have paid:* Lappé, *op. cit.,* p. 85.

133　*fifty-four dollars an acre:* Wuerthner, op. cit.

134　*The biological productivity:* Ibid.

134　*produces only 3 percent of American beef:* Jacobs, op. cit., p. 566.

# ENDNOTES

134  *"Ranching has wasted . . .":* Ibid., p. 3.

135  *some seven hundred million acres:* Ibid., pp. 11–12.

136  *Powerful stockmen allied:* Ibid., p. 17.

136  *federal agencies typically spend more money:* Wuerthner, op. cit.

137  *The government's Animal Damage Control:* Bloyd-Peshkin, Sharon, "Grazing Our Way to Disaster," *Utne Reader,* January/February 1991, pp. 15–16.

137  *enhance the value of private property:* Wuerthner, op. cit.

137  *"The hard truth . . .":* Lessner, Richard, "Dancing with Wolves: Ranchers Should Lose This War," *The Arizona Republic,* April 1, 1991, p. A12.

138  *Seventy-five percent of the 418 million acres:* Jacobs, op. cit., p. 566.

138  *one hundred and eighty-five acres per year:* Ibid., p. 29.

138  *83 percent of its rangeland:* Ibid., p. 31.

138  *six tons of range plant material:* Ibid., p. 34.

139  *highly flammable:* Ibid., p. 37.

139  *"Ecological burdens . . .":* Brown, Lester, *State of the World: 1995,* Worldwatch Institute Report (New York: W. W. Norton, 1995), p. 45.

139  *less than 25 percent of the nitrogen:* Jacobs, op. cit., p. 76.

139  *remain intact for periods of years:* Ibid.

140  *Precious grams of nitrogen:* Ibid., p. 77.

140  *2 percent of their original population:* Kay, Charles, "Leave It to the Beavers," *Montana Magazine,* May/June 1988, pp. 15–16, cited in Jacobs, op. cit., p. 90.

140  *up to 99 percent of aquatic nutrients:* Blumm, Michael, "Livestock Grazing in Riparian Zones: Ensuring Fishery Protection in Federal Rangeland Management,"* Anadromous Fish Law Memo, 1986, cited in Jacobs, op. cit., p. 89.

141  *tens of thousands of Western springs:* Ibid., p. 84.

141  *Eighty to ninety percent of the riparian zones:* Rifkin, op. cit., p. 205.

141  *Eighty-three percent of Wyoming's streams:* Kay, op. cit., cited in Jacobs, op. cit., p. 92.

141  *"Though few people realize it . . .":* Jacobs, op. cit., pp. 49–50.

142  *zero saplings per acre:* Ibid., p. 54.

142  *90 percent of the allotted forage:* Ibid., p. 119.

142  *1 to 3 percent of their primeval population:* Wuerthner, op. cit.

143  *like to hide their newborn in tall grass:* Jacobs, op. cit., p. 117.

143  *bird counts five to seven times higher:* Wuerthner, op. cit.

143  *trout populations to be 350 percent higher:* Ibid.

143  *fastest-disappearing:* Ibid.

143  *103 are grazed:* Ibid.

144  *The diseases livestock spread include:* Jacobs, op. cit., p. 122.

145  *flooding has historically mirrored:* Ibid., p. 104.

145  *tend to be those that are most efficient:* Ibid.

147    *"The thin layer of soil . . .":* Carson, Rachel, *Silent Spring* (Boston: Houghton Mifflin, 1962, 1994) p. 53.

147    *greater extremes in temperature:* Jacobs, op. cit., p. 77.

147    *it can barely support life:* Williams, Florence, "The West's Time Capsules," *High Country News,* March 12, 1990, pp. 6–7, cited in Jacobs, op. cit., p. 69.

147    *the Sahara itself was a region luxuriant:* Cousteau, Jacques, *The Ocean World* (New York: Abradale Press/Harry N. Abrams, 1985), p. 411.

147    *More than one-third:* Jacobs, op. cit., p. 65.

147    *deserts are expanding globally:* Agence France-Presse, September 3, 1997.

148    *the Thar Desert:* Jacobs, op. cit., p. 360.

148    *Scientists speculate:* Ibid., p. 174.

148    *These crusts serve:* Ibid., p. 63.

148    *Even though it takes hundreds of acres:* Ibid., p. 64.

148    *over a hundred ranchers grazing cattle:* Ibid.

148    *the absurd economics:* Ibid.

149    *seven thousand have been detected burning:* Ibid., p. 356.

149    *More of Brazil is aflame now:* "A Rain Forest Imperiled," *New York Times* editorial, October 15, 1997, p. A18.

149    *An area about the size of Maine:* Jacobs, op. cit., p. 356.

149    *An estimated 70 percent:* Ibid.

150    *only 3 to 4 percent of Brazilian beef:* Ibid.

150    *"In San José and Brasília . . .":* Caufield, Catherine, *In the Rainforest* (Chicago: University of Chicago Press, 1986), p. 121.

151    *The forest supports:* Clifford, Frank, "Which Comes First—Food or the Forest?" *Los Angeles Times,* July 24, 1997, p. A1.

151    *Today three hundred thousand people:* Ibid., p. A22.

151    *bare bedrock:* Clifford, Frank, "Quest to Increase Yields by Growing 'Sun Coffee' Fuels Jungle Fires," *Los Angeles Times,* July 24, 1997, p. A23.

151    *More of Mexico's grain:* Jacobs, op. cit., p. 355.

151    *One hundred fifty million cattle:* Ibid., p. 356.

151    *two-thirds of its arable land:* Caufield, op. cit., p. 109.

151    *"One reason . . .":* Ibid., p. 108.

152    *As much as 90 percent:* Park, Chris, *Tropical Rainforests* (London: Routledge, 1992), p. 69.

152    *one person per twelve square miles:* Caufield, op. cit., p. 111.

152    *a hundred people per square mile:* Ibid.

152    *"The developing country . . .":* Park, op. cit., pp. 69–70.

153    *As much as half:* All facts in this paragraph from Jacobs, op. cit., pp. 355–59.

# ENDNOTES

## Chapter Eight: Skip the Miracles and Eat Well

PAGE

154   *weigh about twenty pounds less:* Parham, Vistara, *What's Wrong with Eating Meat?* (Northampton, Mass.: Sisters Universal Publishing, 1979), p. 29.

155   *caused valvular heart disease:* Kolata, Gina, "Companies Recall 2 Top Diet Drugs at F.D.A.'s Urging," *New York Times,* September 16, 1997, pp. A1, A16; Ault, Alicia, "FDA Issues Warning on Diet Drug Combination," *Lancet,* July 19, 1997, p. 189.

155   *as many as 30 percent of those who got suckered:* Kolata, op. cit., p. A1.

156   *30 percent of calories come from fat:* Sears, Barry, and Bill Lawren, *Enter the Zone* (New York: HarperCollins, 1995), p. 72.

156   *"doesn't rob food . . .":* Ibid. p. xvii.

157   *almost as dangerous:* Lecture of Dr. Michael Klaper, Hollywood, California, July 12, 1997.

158   *"You must eat food in a controlled fashion . . .":* Sears and Lawren, op. cit., p. 3.

158   *ice cream:* Ibid., p. 16.

158   *"too many high-glycemic carbohydrates . . .":* Ibid., pp. 17–18.

159   *"varies depending on whether you eat the food cooked . . .":* Raymond, Jennifer, remarks at the North American Vegetarian Summerfest, Johnstown, Pennsylvania, July 11, 1997.

159   *"high levels of insulin . . .":* Sears and Lawren, op. cit., p. 63.

160   *"Vegetable protein tends to be encased . . .":* Ibid., p. 69.

160   *countless studies of the benefits of fiber:* see e.g., Robertson, Sarah, "Natural Cholesterol Cruncher," *Prevention,* November 1996, pp.57–58; Schwade, Steve, and Rao, Linda, "The New Science of Eating to Ease Gut Reactions," *Prevention,* February 1995, pp. 78–80; Munson, Marty, and Yeykal, Teresa, "Bran Loyalty," *Prevention,* May 1995, pp. 22–23; Temple, Norman J., and Burkitt, Denis, *Western Diseases: Their Dietary Prevention and Reversi.bility* (Totowa, N.J.: Humana Press, 1994).

160   *excreted through increased urination:* Sears and Lawren, op. cit., p. 19.

160   *"more than 95% . . .":* Ibid., p. 20.

161   *all but dismisses the role of dietary cholesterol:* Ibid., pp. 141–45.

162   *"the mind is relaxed . . .":* Ibid., p. 1.

163   *To* turkey escalopes fontina: Ibid., p. 91.

164   *"Calories don't count . . .":* Ibid., p. 67.

165   *"But what about total calories . . .":* Ibid., pp. 75–76.

166   *The EMI for Cheddar cheese:* This and succeeding facts about the EMI from Marcus, Erik, *Vegan: The New Ethics of Eating* (Ithaca, N.Y.: McBooks Press, 1997), pp. 43–53.

168   *"Calories from carbohydrates . . .":* Barnard, Neal D., *Physician's Slimming Guide* (Summertown, Tenn.: Book Publishing Company, 1992), p. 15.

168    *carbohydrates boost metabolism:* Ibid.

168    *such labels are misleading:* Robbins, John, *Diet for a New America* (Walpole, N.H.: Stillpoint Publishing, 1987) p. 235.

168    *Milk labeled 2 percent fat is actually:* Barnard, op. cit., p. 21.

169    *ground beef provides about 54 percent:* This and succeeding fat percentages from Ibid.., pp. 21–25.

170    *Exercising frequently in moderation: ABC Evening News,* November 11, 1997.

170    Greene, Bob, and Oprah Winfrey, *Make the Connection* (New York: Hyperion, 1996).

171    *"The New Four Food Groups":* Barnard, op. cit., pp. 59–61.

179    *genistein, found in soybeans, inhibits the growth of tumors:* Angier, Natalie, "Chemists Learn Why Vegetables Are Good for You," *New York Times,* April 13, 1993, p. C1.

179    *saponins, a class of compounds found in fruits and vegetables:* Lipkin, Richard, "Vegemania: Scientists Tout the Health Benefits of Saponins," *Science News,* vol. 148, December 9, 1995, pp. 392–93; "Bodyguards for the Twenty-first Century," Lustgarden, Steve, *EarthSave International Newsletter,* Fall 1997, vol. 8, no. 3, pp. 1–5.

179    *"The truth is that the more researchers understand . . .":* Angier, Natalie, op. cit., p. C1.

180    *a rare disease called homocystinuria:* McCully, Kilmer S., *The Homocysteine Revolution* (New Canaan, Conn.: Keats Publishing, 1997), p. 2.

180    *perhaps homocysteine, rather than cholesterol, is the active agent:* McCully, op. cit.; Gruberg, Edward R., and Stephen A. Raymond, *Beyond Cholesterol* (New York: St. Martin's Press, 1981).

180    *serum homocysteine levels mirror risk of cardiac arrest:* Stampfer, M. J., et al., "A Prospective Study of Plasma Homocysteine and Risk of Myocardial Infarction in U.S. Physicians," *Journal of the American Medical Association,* 268:877–81, cited in Barnard, Neal, *The Power of Your Plate* (Summertown, Tenn.: Book Publishing Company, 1995), p. 144.

181    *2 micrograms per day:* Barnard, *The Power of Your Plate,* p. 197.

183    *How do humans compare:* Parham, op. cit., pp. 2–8.

183    *"has no curved beak, no sharp talons . . .":* Plutarch, "Essay on Flesh Eating," from "Morals," cited in Spencer, Colin, *The Heretic's Feast: A History of Vegetarianism* (Hanover, N.H.: University Press of New England, 1995), p. 100.

## Chapter Nine: Going Home

PAGE

187    *estimated at $28 to $61 billion annualy:* Barnard, Neal D., Nicholson, Andrew, and Howard, Jo Lil, "The Medical Costs Attributable to Meet Consumption," *Preventive Medicine,* vol. 24, 1995, pp. 646–55.

# BIBLIOGRAPHY

## Recommended Reading

Akers, Keith, *A Vegetarian Sourcebook: The Nutrition, Ecology, and Ethics of a Natural Foods Diet* (Vegetarian Press, 1993).

Attwood, Charles, *Dr. Attwood's Low-Fat Prescription for Kids* (Viking, 1995).

Barker, Rodney, *And the Waters Turned to Blood* (Simon & Schuster, 1997).

Barnard, Neal, *Eat Right, Live Longer* (Crown, 1995).

——, *Food for Life* (Harmony Books, 1993).

——, *A Physician's Slimming Guide* (The Book Publishing Co., 1992).

——, *The Power of Your Plate* (The Book Publishing Co., 1995).

Boyd, Billy Ray, *For the Vegetarian in You* (Prima Publishing, 1996).

Burkitt, Dennis, and Temple, Norman, *Western Diseases* (Humana Press, 1994).

Burwash, Peter, *Total Health* (Torchlight Publishing, Inc., 1997).

Campbell, T. Colin, *The China Project* (New Century Nutrition, 1996).

Carson, Rachel, *Silent Spring* (Houghton Mifflin, 1962). The book that began the modern environmental movement.

Caufield, Catherine, *In the Rainforest* (University of Chicago Press, 1984).

Coe, Sue, and Cockburn, Alexander, *Dead Meat* (Four Walls Eight Windows, 1995).

Cox, Peter, *Guide to Vegetarian Living* (Bloomsbury Publishing, 1995).

——, *The New Why You Don't Need Meat* (Bloomsbury Publishing, 1992).

Davis, Gail, *So, Now What Do I Eat?* (Blue Coyote Press, 1998).

Diamond, Harvey and Marilyn, *Fit for Life* (Warner Books, 1987).

Eisman, George, *The Most Noble Diet* (Diet Ethics, 1994).

Fox, Michael W., *Agricide* (Schocken Books, 1986).

——, *The Boundless Circle* (Quest Books, 1996).

——, *Eating with Conscience* (New Sage Press, 1997).

Greene, Bob, and Winfrey, Oprah, *Make the Connection* (Hyperion, 1996).

Harris, William, *The Scientific Basis of Vegetarianism* (Hawaii Health Publisher, 1995).

Hitchcox, Lee, *Long Life Now* (Celestial Hearts, 1996).

Jacobs, Lynn, *Waste of the West* (Lynn Jacobs, 1991. To order: 520-791-2913, or P.O. Box 5784, Tucson, AZ, 85703.

Klaper, Michael, *Pregnancy, Children and the Vegan Diet* (Gentle World, 1988).

——, *Vegan Nutrition: Pure and Simple* (Gentle World, 1987).

Kradjian, Robert, *Save Yourself from Breast Cancer* (Berkley Publishing Group, 1994).

Krebs, A. V., *The Corporate Reapers* (Essential Books, 1992).

Kushi, Michio, *The Cancer Prevention Diet* (St. Martin's Press, 1994).

# BIBLIOGRAPHY

Lacey, Richard W., *Mad Cow Disease: The History of BSE in Britain* (Cypsela Publications, 1994).

Langley, Gill, *Vegan Nutrition* (Vegan Society UK, 1995).

Lappé, Frances Moore, *Diet for a Small Planet* (Ballantine, 1991).

Lappé, Frances Moore, and Collins, Joseph, *Food First* (Houghton Mifflin, 1977).

Marcus, Erik, *Vegan: The New Ethics of Eating* (McBooks Press, 1997).

Mason, Jim, and Singer, Peter, *Animal Factories* (Harmony Books, 1980).

McDougall, John, *The McDougall Program for a Healthy Heart* (Dutton, 1996).

——, *The McDougall Program for Maximum Weight Loss* (Penguin Books, 1994).

McDougall, John, and McDougall, Mary, *The McDougall Program: 12 Days to Dynamic Health* (Penguin Books, 1990).

Messina, Mark and Virginia, *The Vegetarian Way* (Three Rivers Press, 1996).

Ornish, Dean, *Dr. Dean Ornish's Program for Reversing Heart Disease* (Ballantine, 1990).

——, *Eat More, Weigh Less* (HarperCollins, 1993).

Park, Chris, *Tropical Rainforests* (Routledge, 1992).

Pinckney, Neal, *Healthy Heart* (Health Communications, Inc., 1996).

Rampton, Sheldon, and Stauber, John, *Mad Cow U.S.A.: Could the Nightmare Happen Here?* (Common Courage Press, 1997).

Rhodes, Richard, *Deadly Feasts* (Simon & Schuster, 1997).

Rifkin, Jeremy, *Beyond Beef* (Penguin Books, 1992).

Robbins, John, *Diet for a New America* (Stillpoint Publishing, 1987). To order: (800) 847-4014. A classic.

——, *May All Be Fed* (William Morrow, 1992).

——, *Reclaiming Our Health* (H. J. Kramer, 1996).

Robbins, Ocean, and Solomon, Sol, *Choices for Our Future* (Book Publishing Company, 1994).

Spencer, Colin, *The Heretic's Feast* (University Press of New England, 1995).

Twogood, Daniel, *No Milk* (Wilhelmina Books, 1991).

*Vegetarian Journal's Guide to Natural Foods Restaurants in the U.S. and Canada* (Vegetarian Resource Group, 1993).

Whitaker, Julian M., *Reversing Heart Disease* (Warner Books, 1985).

## Cookbooks

Atlas, Nava, *Vegetariana* (Little, Brown and Co., 1984).

Curlee, Sue, *From Sue With Love* (From Sue With Love Books, 1996).

Diamond, Marilyn, *The American Vegetarian Cookbook* (Random House, 1990).

Emmons, Didi, *Vegetarian Planet* (Harvard Common Press, 1997).

Ettinger, John, *101 Meatless Family Dishes:* (Prima, 1995).

Hagler, Louise, *The Farm Vegetarian Cookbook* (Book Publishing Company, 1994).

Hoshijo, Kathy, *Kathy Cooks–Vegetarian, Low Cholesterol* (Simon & Schuster, 1989).

# Bibliography

Jaffrey, Madhur, *Madhur Jaffrey's World of the Past Vegetarian Cuisine* (Alfred A. Knopf, 1989).

Katzen, Mollie, *The Moosewood Cookbook* (Ten Speed Press, 1992).

McCartney, Linda, *Linda McCartney's Home Cooking* (Arcade, 1990).

McCarty, Meredith, *Fresh from a Vegetarian Kitchen* (St. Martin's Press, 1995).

Madison, Deborah, *Vegetarian Cooking for Everyone* (Broadway Books).

Melina, Vesanto, and Davis, Brenda and Harrison, *Becoming Vegetarian* (Macmillan Canada, 1994).

Nearing, Helen, *Simple Food for the Good Life* (Stillpoint Publishing, 1985).

Newkirk, Ingrid, *The Compassionate Cook* (Warner Books, 1993).

Nishimoto, Miyoko, *TheNow and Zen Epicure: Gourmet Cuisine for the Enlightened Palate* (Book Publishing Company, 1991).

Pickarski, Brother Ron, *Friendly Foods: Gourmet Vegetarian Cuisine* (Ten Speed Press, 1991).

Raymond, Jennifer, *Fat Free & Easy: Great Meals in Minutes* (Book Publishing Company, 1997).

——, *The Peaceful Palate: Fine Vegetarian Cuisine* (Book Publishing Company, 1996).

Robertson, Laurel, Flinders, Carol, and Ruppenthal, Brian, *The New Laurel's Kitchen* (Ten Speed Press, 1996).

Sass, Lorna, *Recipes from an Ecological Kitchen* (William Morrow, 1992).

Stepaniak, Joanne, *The Uncheese Cookbook* (Book Publishing Company, 1994).

——, *Vegan Vittles* (Book Publishing Company, 1996).

Stepaniak, Joanne, and Hecker, Cathy, *Ecological Cooking: Recipes to Save the Planet* (Book Publishing Company, 1992).

Thomas, Anna, *The Vegetarian Epicure* (Random House, 1972).

*Vegetarian Times Complete Cookbook* (Vegetarian Times Bookshelf, 1995).

Wagner, Lindsay, and Spade, Ariane, *The High Road to Health: A Vegetarian Cookbook* (Simon & Schuster, 1990).

Wasserman, Debra, *Conveniently Vegan* (Vegetarian Resource Group, 1997).

——, *The Lowfat Jewish Vegetarian Cookbook: Healthy Traditions from Around the World* (Vegetarian Resource Group, 1995).

——, *No Cholesterol Passover Recipes* (Vegetarian Resource Group, 1995).

Wasserman, Debra, and Mangels, R., *Simply Vegan* (Vegetarian Resource Group, 1995).

Wasserman, Debra, and Stahler, Charles, *Meatless Meals for Working People* (Vegetarian Resource Group, 1991).

## Organizations; Networking Resources

American Natural Hygiene Society
12816 Race Track Road
Tampa, FL 33625
(813) 855-6607

# BIBLIOGRAPHY

American Vegan Society
P.O. Box H
Malaga, NJ 08328
(609) 694-2887

EarthSave International
620 B Distillery Commons
Louisville, KY 40206
(502) 589-7676

Eating with Conscience Campaign
Humane Society of the United States
700 Professional Drive
Gaithersburg, MD 20879
(301) 258-3054

Farm Animal Reform Movement (FARM)
Box 30654
Bethesda, MD 20879
(301) 530-5747

Farm Sanctuary East
P.O. Box 150
Watkins Glen, NY 14891
(607) 583-2225

Farm Sanctuary West
P.O. Box 1065
Orland, CA 95963
(916) 865-4617

Friends Vegetarian Society of North America (Quaker)
P.O. Box 53354
Washington, DC 20009

International Vegetarian Union
P.O. Box 22903
Alexandria, VA 22304

Jewish Vegetarians of North America
6938 Reliance Road
Federalsburg, MD 21632
(410) 754-5550

North American Vegetarian Society
P.O. Box 72
Dolgeville, NY 13329
(518) 568-7970

People for the Ethical Treatment of Animals (PETA)
501 Front Street
Norfolk, VA 23570
(757) 622-1078

Physicians Committee for Responsible Medicine (PCRM)
5100 Wisconsin Ave., NW, Suite 404
Washington, DC 20016
(202) 686-2210

Rainforest Action Network
221 Pine St., Suite 500
San Francisco, CA 94104
(415) 398-4404

Sierra Club
85 Second St., 2nd floor
San Francisco, CA 94105
(415) 977-5500

United Poultry Concerns
P.O. Box 59367
Potomac, MD 20859
(301) 948-2406

Vegan Action
P.O. Box 4353
Berkeley, CA 94704
(510) 654-6297

Vegedine–Association of Vegetarian Dietitians & Nutrition Educators
3835 Route 414
Burdette, NY 14818
(607) 546-7171

Vegetarian Awareness Network
P.O. Box 321
Knoxville, TN 37901
(800) EAT-VEGE

# BIBLIOGRAPHY

Vegetarian Resource Group
P.O. Box 1463
Baltimore, MD 21203
(410) 366-VEGE

Vegetarian Society, Inc.
P.O. Box 34427
Los Angeles, CA 90034
(310) 559-9769

Vegetarian Union of North America (VUNA)
P.O. Box 9710
Washington, DC 20016
(617) 625-3790

Voice for a Viable Future
11288 Ventura Blvd., #202A
Studio City, CA 91604
(818) 509-1255

## Internet Sites

Animal Rights Resource Site
http://www.envirolink.org/arrs/

BioSpirituality
http://www.vegsource.org/biospirituality/

Charles Attwood, M.D.
http://www.vegsource.org/attwood/

EarthSave International
http://www.earthsave.org

Farm Animal Reform Movement (FARM)
http://www.envirolink.org/arrs/farm/

Farm Sanctuary
http://www.farmsanctuary.org/

Ruth Heidrich, Ph.D.
http://www.vegsource.org/heidrich/

The Jewish Vegan Lifestyle
http://www.goodnet.com/~tjvmab/

Michael Klaper, M.D.
http://www.vegsource.org/klaper/

Howard Lyman
http://www.vegsource.org/lyman/

New Veg
http://www.newveg.av.org/

North American Vegetarian Society (NAVS)
http://www.cyberveg.org/navs

People for the Ethical Treatment of Animals (PETA)
http://envirolink.org/arrs/peta/index.html

Physicians' Committee for Reponsible Medicine (PCRM)
http://sai.com/pcrm/

Vegan Action
http://www.vegan.org/

Vegan Outreach
http://www.vegsource.org/vo/

Vegetarian Pages
http://www.veg.org/veg/

Vegetarian Resource Group
http://www.vrg.org/

Vegetarian Society U.K.
http://www.veg.org/veg/Orgs/VegSocUK/

Vegetarian Union of North America (VUNA)
http://www.ivu.org/vuna/

Vegetarian Youth Network
http://www.geocities.com/RodeoDrive/1154/

Veggies Unite!
http://www.vegweb.com/

VegSource
http://www.vegsource.com/

World Guide to Vegetarianism
http://catless.ncl.ac.uk/veg/Guide/

## Magazines and Newsletters

*McDougall Newsletter*
John McDougall, M.D.
P.O. Box 14039
Santa Rosa, CA 95402

# BIBLIOGRAPHY

*Vegetarian Journal*
(published by Vegetarian Resource Group)
(410) 366-8343

*Vegetarian Times*
P.O. Box 570
Oak Park, IL 60303
(708) 848-8100

*Vegetarian Voice*
(published by North American Vegetarian Society)
(518) 568-7970

# INDEX

Abortion, 122
Acromegaly, 111
Agent Orange, 53
Agriculture, U.S. Department of,
    20, 38, 74, 79, 98
  antibiotics regulations of, 110
  author's study of files of, 98–99
  data on new product wanted by,
    106–7
  growers protected by, 58
  U.S. Forest Service under, 136–38
AIDS, 96
Air pollution from raising beef,
    124–28
Alper, Tikvah, 85
Alzheimer's disease, 100
American Diabetes Association,
    159
American Farm Bureau Federation,
    82
American Heart Association, 27
Anemia, 36, 181, 182
Angier, Natalie, 179
Animal Damage Control division,
    137
Animal feed
  blood products in, 101
  European ban on products in, 101
  excrement in, 12, 13
  grain diverted to, 42–43
  protein concentrates in, 12, 54
  scrapie-infected sheep-remains in,
    83, 85–89, 98, 100
Animals, wild, cattle's destruction
    of, 142–44
Animal shelters, euthanized pets
    from, 12
Antibiotics
  for beef cattle, 55–56
  for dairy cows, 110–11

Aquifer, Ogallala, 132–33
Argentina, overgrazing in, 151
Arizona, 141
  livestock water usage in, 131
  political power of ranchers in, 136
Arthritis, 36
Association for the Advancement
    of Science, 31
Atherosclerosis, 23, 24, 28, 177
Atkins diet, 161
Australia, 153
Avocados, 169

*Babe* (movie), 16
Barbasco vine, 151
Barker, Rodney, 129
Barnard, Neal, 168, 171
Beef
  air pollution from raising of,
    124–28
  amount of cholesterol in, 37
  in developing world, 43, 80
  European ban on American, 58
  "extra-lean" ground, 169
  federal regulations on ground, 98
  inefficiency of production of, 41
  Latin American exports of,
    152–53
  rain forest destruction and,
    149–50
  ranch-raised, 133–36
Beef Promotion Council, 16
Ben & Jerry's, 117
Beyond Beef campaign, 98
Biological pest and weed control,
    73–74
Biomass, destruction of, 124
Birth control pill, 151
Bolivia, overgrazing in, 151
Bone cancer, 113

# INDEX

*Index*